Happy M̶̶̶
Sweety Betty.

May these little
daily devotions speak
to your heart and
fill you with Joy.
Thank You for your
genuine kindness.
Our Love,
Justin, Angel, Aspen
and Austin

One-Minute
INSPIRATIONS
for WOMEN

Publications International, Ltd.

Writer: Caroline Delbert

Cover and interior art: Shutterstock.com,
except page 16, 21, 125 from Getty

Louis Weber, CEO
Publications International, Ltd.
8140 Lehigh Avenue
Morton Grove, IL 60053

ISBN: 978-1-68022-757-4

Manufactured in China.

8 7 6 5 4 3 2 1

You Only Need a Minute

*God is love, and he loves the lover.
His intrinsic nature compels him
to answer the call of his beloved.*
— *Russell H. Conwell*

In the rush and chaos of daily life, a minute — a full minute! — can sound luxurious. *One-Minute Inspirations for Women* is designed to give you maximum value for your minute, including scripture, quotes, and brief reflections. Think of each entry as a spark, the catalyst to inspire you and set the tone for the rest of your day.

Inspiration originally meant to breathe in, like respiration but directly from the gods. A steady, deep breath can clear and refresh your mind. Let these passages and prayers breathe new spiritual life into your busy routine.

And when they had prayed, the place was shaken where they were assembled together; and they were all filled with the Holy Ghost, and they spake the word of God with boldness.

— *Acts 4:31*

There are days when we feel confident, assured, and emboldened. It's tempting to say, "This is my lucky day!" But with God, every day is lucky, and there's no luck involved. He emboldens us. We reach for him and he gives us strength.

But do thou for me, O God the Lord,
for thy name's sake:
because thy mercy is good, deliver thou me.
— Psalms 109:21

Psalm 109 is a scorcher, famous for its salt-the-earth language about one's enemies. Its author reaches for God to confirm his faith and prove those enemies wrong. God sets an example of mercy and charity that we can easily spend our lives trying to emulate. To always be kind and generous is an intimidating idea, but to make one kind or generous choice at a time is so doable.

*They bowed themselves with their faces
to the ground upon the pavement,
and worshipped, and praised the Lord,
saying, For he is good;
for his mercy endureth for ever.*
— 2 Chronicles 7:3

Solomon appears in so much of the Old Testament, casting a long shadow as a wise, powerful, wealthy leader favored by God. Even so, he and his people have sins and flaws to atone for. The most powerful people still have to answer to God, but they can also ask for God's help. Solomon acts as a role model for his people.

Little children, yet a little while I am with you. Ye shall seek me: and as I said unto the Jews, Whither I go, ye cannot come; so now I say to you. A new commandment I give unto you, That ye love one another; as I have loved you, that ye also love one another.

— John 13:33–34

The simplest idea can be the most challenging to really do. On our busiest days, we must love one another. In our most trying times, we must still love one another. With no caveats or excuses, we must always love one another. We can work to make this love easier to find in ourselves by being appreciative, grateful, and humble during our best times — stockpiling those feelings like a rainy-day fund.

For we know him that hath said,
Vengeance belongeth unto me,
I will recompense, saith the Lord. And again,
The Lord shall judge his people.
It is a fearful thing to fall into the hands
of the living God.
— Hebrews 10:30–31

Only God can judge — we all know this cornerstone of scripture and do our flawed best to honor it. But how interesting to think of "the living God." When Jesus Christ was on Earth, his disciples not only learned from his example; they made choices and lived their lives in his presence. Imagine if God were standing, bodily, next to every person you met. How might you act differently?

Hear the right, O Lord,
attend unto my cry, give ear unto my prayer,
that goeth not out of feigned lips.

— *Psalms 17:1*

Every adult has likely seen a kid tell a bad lie: "I'm too sick to go to school," or maybe "I don't know who broke the vase." There may as well be a neon sign, because most children don't have the skills that let adults tell much more convincing lies to each other. Take a minute to clear your heart of clutter before you go to God, and be honest with him and yourself.

And I will cleanse them from all their iniquity, whereby they have sinned against me; and I will pardon all their iniquities, whereby they have sinned, and whereby they have transgressed against me.

— Jeremiah 33:8

How can we put others' mistakes in perspective? God not only forgives the sin but understands the heart of the sinner. We tiny mortals can try to do the same!

Save, Lord: let the king hear us when we call.
— Psalms 20:9

*I have called upon thee, for thou wilt
hear me, O God: incline thine ear unto me,
and hear my speech.*
— Psalms 17:6

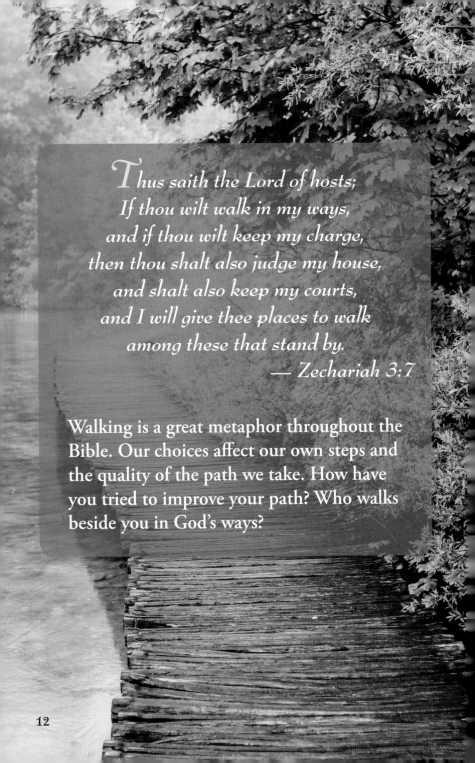

Thus saith the Lord of hosts;
If thou wilt walk in my ways,
and if thou wilt keep my charge,
then thou shalt also judge my house,
and shalt also keep my courts,
and I will give thee places to walk
among these that stand by.
— Zechariah 3:7

Walking is a great metaphor throughout the Bible. Our choices affect our own steps and the quality of the path we take. How have you tried to improve your path? Who walks beside you in God's ways?

I will pay thee my vows,
Which my lips have uttered,
and my mouth hath spoken,
when I was in trouble.
— Psalms 66:13–14

Crisis bargains with God are played for laughs or tears in movies, but in real life, these prayers can help us out of some serious jams. It's important to be thankful for the help we receive, whether it's a last-minute medical miracle or simply the calm we need to face the day.

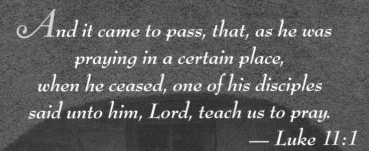

And it came to pass, that, as he was praying in a certain place, when he ceased, one of his disciples said unto him, Lord, teach us to pray.

— Luke 11:1

Think of life as a long series of opportunities to set a good example for others. To love your neighbor as you love yourself includes sharing your best "trade secrets" for anyone to use. The disciples watched Jesus in private prayer and reflection and asked him to be a role model for them.

*Take quiet time, and be still before God,
that He may take this matter in hand.
Leave yourself in God's hands.*
— *Rev. Andrew Murray*

For I will take you from among the heathen, and gather you out of all countries, and will bring you into your own land. Then will I sprinkle clean water upon you, and ye shall be clean: from all your filthiness, and from all your idols, will I cleanse you. A new heart also will I give you, and a new spirit will I put within you: and I will take away the stony heart out of your flesh, and I will give you an heart of flesh. And I will put my spirit within you, and cause you to walk in my statutes, and ye shall keep my judgments, and do them. And ye shall dwell in the land that I gave to your fathers; and ye shall be my people, and I will be your God.

— Ezekiel 36:24–28

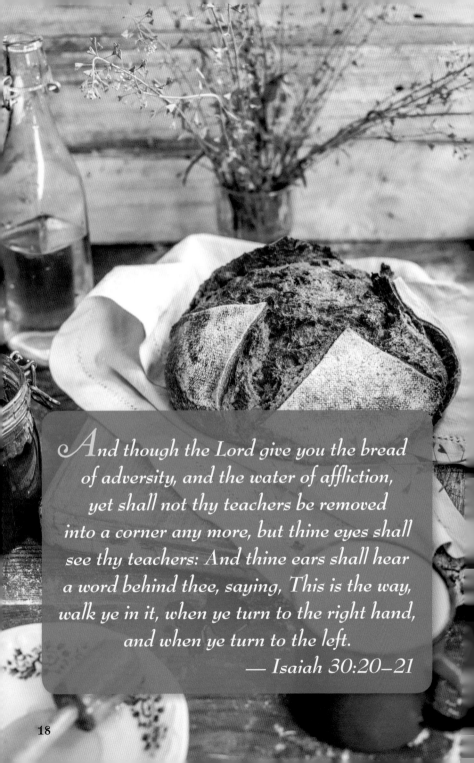

And though the Lord give you the bread of adversity, and the water of affliction, yet shall not thy teachers be removed into a corner any more, but thine eyes shall see thy teachers: And thine ears shall hear a word behind thee, saying, This is the way, walk ye in it, when ye turn to the right hand, and when ye turn to the left.

— Isaiah 30:20–21

18

*And I will strengthen them in the Lord;
and they shall walk up and down in his name,
saith the Lord.*

— Zechariah 10:12

How has God's strength shown itself in your life? Do you ask for God's help when you need it?

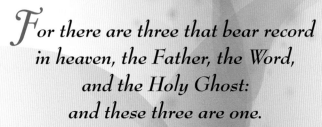

For there are three that bear record in heaven, the Father, the Word, and the Holy Ghost: and these three are one.

— *1 John 5:7*

Were there skeptics in your childhood math classes who asked questions like, "How can infinity plus one still be infinity?" The fact of the Trinity is a cause for awe and wonder, not skepticism.

*God offers Himself, gives Himself away,
to the whole-hearted who give themselves
wholly away to Him.
He always gives us according to
our heart's desire.
But not as we think it, but as He sees it.*
— Rev. Andrew Murray

*I will not leave you comfortless:
I will come to you.*

— *John 14:18*

*And they prayed, and said, Thou, Lord,
which knowest the hearts of all men,
shew whether of these two thou hast chosen.*

— *Acts 1:24*

Sing, O heavens; and be joyful, O earth; and break forth into singing, O mountains: for the Lord hath comforted his people, and will have mercy upon his afflicted.

— Isaiah 49:13

Isaiah wants his prophecy of mercy and joy to be contagious for all of creation: the people as well as the heavens and the mountains. It's a touching counterpoint to the times when God shakes the earth to show his people the error of their ways. Isaiah's prophecy, echoing Psalm 100, reminds us to express our gratitude and love to God.

Let us have grace, whereby
we may serve God acceptably
with reverence and godly fear:
For our God is a consuming fire.
— *Hebrews 12:28–29*

John Donne famously used the metaphor of
God as fire and wrote that God can "break,
blow, burn, and make me new." We are torn
down and built back up by the fire, and, like
pottery, we are stronger for it.

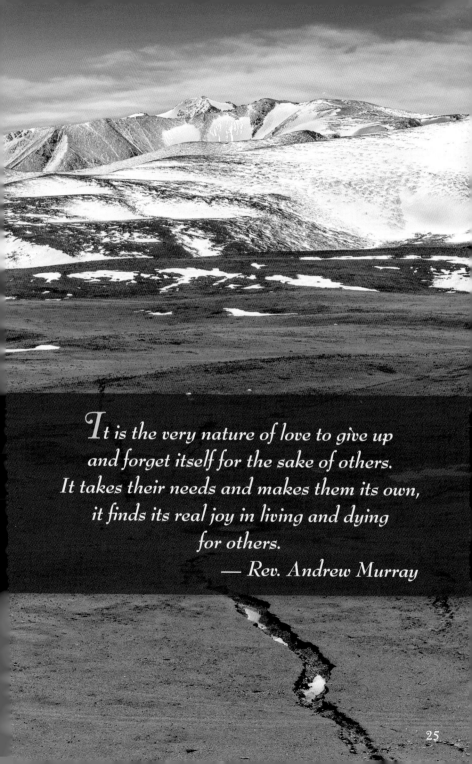

*I*t is the very nature of love to give up
and forget itself for the sake of others.
It takes their needs and makes them its own,
it finds its real joy in living and dying
for others.
— Rev. Andrew Murray

*I*s any thing too hard for the Lord?
— *Genesis 18:14*

*R*emember them that are in bonds,
as bound with them;
and them which suffer adversity,
as being yourselves also in the body.
— *Hebrews 13:3*

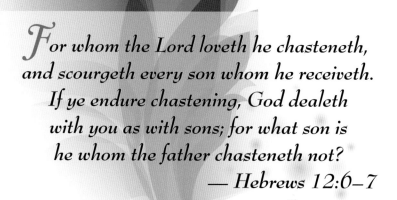

*For whom the Lord loveth he chasteneth,
and scourgeth every son whom he receiveth.
If ye endure chastening, God dealeth
with you as with sons; for what son is
he whom the father chasteneth not?*
— Hebrews 12:6–7

God sets an example of all-encompassing
love that includes discipline. We struggle
when our children or other family members
misbehave or when coworkers treat us badly.
Is there someone in your life you should
treat more strictly? Is there someone to
whom you should express your needs
more clearly?

$\mathcal{A}$nd the Lord said unto Moses,
Whosoever hath sinned against me,
him will I blot out of my book.
Therefore now go, lead the people
unto the place of which I have spoken
unto thee: behold, mine Angel shall go
before thee: nevertheless in the day
when I visit I will visit their sin upon them.

— *Exodus 32:33–34*

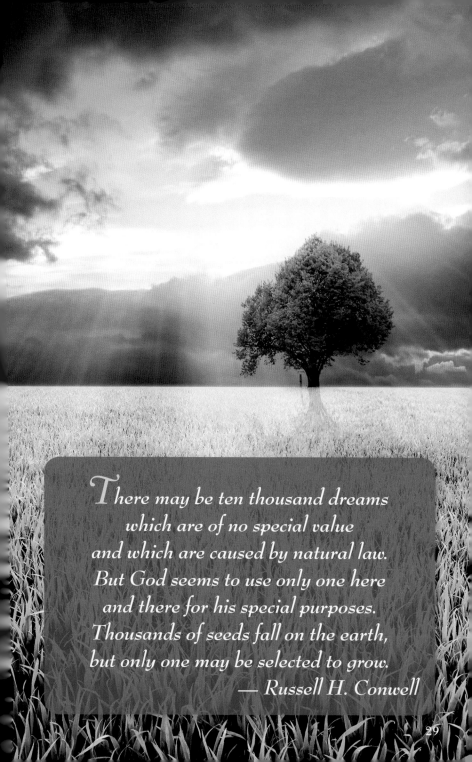

*There may be ten thousand dreams
which are of no special value
and which are caused by natural law.
But God seems to use only one here
and there for his special purposes.
Thousands of seeds fall on the earth,
but only one may be selected to grow.*

— *Russell H. Conwell*

The Lord is my helper, and I will not fear what man shall do unto me.

— Hebrews 13:6

Is there a tough "worldly" problem in the back of your mind that could be solved or resolved by gathering up your courage? God is beside you. Together, you can free up that mental real estate for better uses.

ℱor thus saith the Lord;
Like as I have brought all this great evil
upon this people, so will I bring upon them
all the good that I have promised them.
                              — Jeremiah 32:42

We have countless adages about the balance
of good and bad in our lives, but remember
to also think about consistency. Human
history is one long string of God's promises
of both punishment and reward. To be
reliable in your own life helps to foster the
kind of trust we share with God.

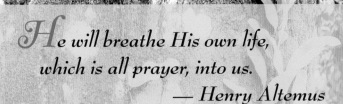

He will breathe His own life,
which is all prayer, into us.
— Henry Altemus

Hear the word of the Lord,
ye rulers of Sodom;
give ear unto the law of our God,
ye people of Gomorrah.
— Isaiah 1:10

*I will pray with the spirit, and I will pray
with the understanding also:
I will sing with the spirit,
and I will sing with the understanding also.*
— *1 Corinthians 14:15*

The adage "Be careful what you wish for"
is taken as a caution, but it's also good
advice. The same prayer can come from a
place of selflessness or of pride, and the
difference is not only clear to God, it affects
how we approach God in the first place.
Pray with care and with a clear conscience.
Be frank with God and be ready to receive
a frank response.

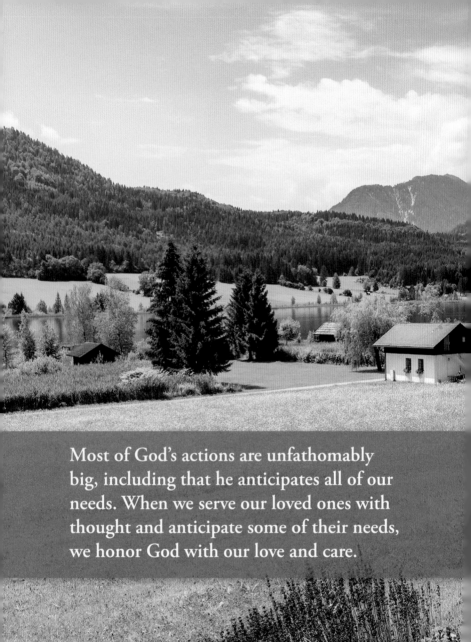

Most of God's actions are unfathomably big, including that he anticipates all of our needs. When we serve our loved ones with thought and anticipate some of their needs, we honor God with our love and care.

But thou, when thou prayest,
enter into thy closet,
and when thou hast shut thy door,
pray to thy Father which is in secret;
and thy Father which seeth
in secret shall reward thee openly.
— Matthew 6:6

Public life can feel like a performance, but prayer is simple and discreet, as laid out in Matthew 6. Don't say more than you need to say, and don't ask for more than you need to ask for. Speak plainly and with reverence. Pray in a place where you feel comfortable.

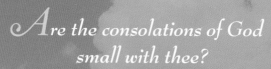

*A*re the consolations of God
small with thee?
— *Job 15:11*

*R*eturn, ye backsliding children,
and I will heal your backslidings.
Behold, we come unto thee;
for thou art the Lord our God.
— *Jeremiah 3:22*

Our fathers trusted in thee:
they trusted, and thou didst deliver them.
They cried unto thee, and were delivered:
they trusted in thee,
and were not confounded.
— Psalms 22:4–5

In Psalm 22, a desperate believer cries out
to God. His pleas reflect his absolute faith:
God, I know you help everyone who trusts
in you — what more can I do to deserve the
help I know you're offering?

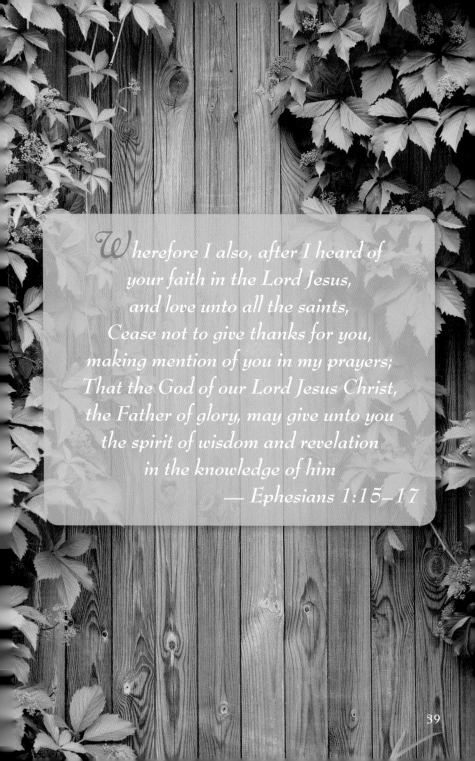

*Wherefore I also, after I heard of
your faith in the Lord Jesus,
and love unto all the saints,
Cease not to give thanks for you,
making mention of you in my prayers;
That the God of our Lord Jesus Christ,
the Father of glory, may give unto you
the spirit of wisdom and revelation
in the knowledge of him*
— *Ephesians 1:15–17*

And whatsoever we ask, we receive of him,
because we keep his commandments,
and do those things that are pleasing
in his sight.

— 1 John 3:22

Here John means both the formal
commandments and Christ's constant
refrain that we must love one another in
thoughts and actions. Which of the two
sounds more daunting to you?

*It is so true that "God will be
no man's debtor." When he asks for
and receives our all, he gives in return
that which is above price—his own presence.
The price is not great when compared
with what he gives in return;
it is our blindness and our unwillingness
to yield that make it seem great.*

— Rosalind Goforth

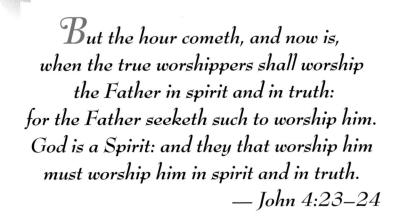

*But the hour cometh, and now is,
when the true worshippers shall worship
the Father in spirit and in truth:
for the Father seeketh such to worship him.
God is a Spirit: and they that worship him
must worship him in spirit and in truth.*

— John 4:23–24

*Grant thee according to thine own heart,
and fulfil all thy counsel.*

— Psalms 20:4

*Only fear the Lord, and serve him in truth
with all your heart: for consider
how great things he hath done for you.*

— 1 Samuel 12:24

I thank God, whom I serve from
my forefathers with pure conscience,
that without ceasing I have remembrance
of thee in my prayers night and day.
— 2 Timothy 1:3

What kinder thing could Paul possibly
write to his dear friend Timothy than that
he prays without ceasing for him in the
same breath that he thanks God? Their deep
friendship was founded in their shared
spiritual path.

*F*or we are his workmanship,
created in Christ Jesus unto good works,
which God hath before ordained
that we should walk in them.
— *Ephesians 2:10*

Think about a person who helped to guide you to follow in God's footsteps, or perhaps guided you back to them after you'd wandered off the path. Who helped that person find their way to God? Even now, thousands of years later, following Christ involves the same word of mouth as the epistle to the Ephesians.

45

Meditate upon these things;
give thyself wholly to them;
that thy profiting may appear to all.
Take heed unto thyself,
and unto the doctrine;
continue in them:
for in doing this thou shalt both save thyself,
and them that hear thee.
— 1 Timothy 4:15–16

*Pray on, dear one—
the power lies that way.*

— Mary Slessor

*After two days will he revive us:
in the third day he will raise us up,
and we shall live in his sight.*

— Hosea 6:2

Let the word of Christ dwell in you richly
in all wisdom; teaching and admonishing
one another in psalms and hymns
and spiritual songs, singing with grace
in your hearts to the Lord.
And whatsoever ye do in word or deed,
do all in the name of the Lord Jesus,
giving thanks to God and the Father by him.
— Colossians 3:16–17

A good and wise father must often deny his child the article for which he asks, but he will not dismiss the matter with a curt denial. He will try to find something else for his child.

— Russell H. Conwell

I the Lord do keep it;
I will water it every moment:
lest any hurt it,
I will keep it night and day.
— Isaiah 27:3

To nurture is a constant job. God's ever-present attention gives us the tools we need but we must choose to take those tools and grow toward the sun of his love.

*Then he turned his face to the wall,
and prayed unto the Lord, saying,
I beseech thee, O Lord, remember now
how I have walked before thee in truth
and with a perfect heart, and have done
that which is good in thy sight.*
— *2 Kings 20:2–4*

Hezekiah's deathbed prayer foretold many of the guidelines Jesus Christ later gave to the Apostles. The prayer was short and direct, spoken humbly and in a private place. God answered Hezekiah's prayer by adding years to his life.

$\mathcal{D}$eal bountifully with thy servant,
that I may live, and keep thy word.
— Psalms 119:17

$\mathcal{A}$t that day ye shall ask in my name:
and I say not unto you,
that I will pray the Father for you.
— John 16:26

Yea, the darkness hideth not from thee;
but the night shineth as the day:
the darkness and the light are both alike
to thee. For thou hast possessed my reins:
thou hast covered me in my mother's womb.
— Psalms 139:12–13

*T*herefore I say unto you,
What things soever ye desire,
when ye pray, believe that ye receive them,
and ye shall have them.
— Mark 11:24

Children have an advantage in their
relationship with God, because their
thoughts are more clear and their
conviction more pure. As an adult, with so
many obligations and complications, how
do you quiet your other worries and doubts
in order to talk to God with a clear mind?

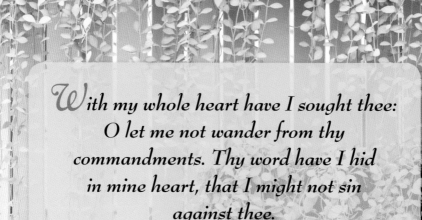

*With my whole heart have I sought thee:
O let me not wander from thy
commandments. Thy word have I hid
in mine heart, that I might not sin
against thee.*
— *Psalms 119:10–11*

Practice makes perfect, especially with God.
If someone asked, could you list the ten
commandments, or explain the context of
one of his miracles in the Gospel of John?
We often memorize frivolous things without
meaning to — maybe that energy can be
redirected into something more worthwhile.

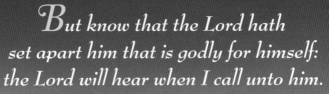

*But know that the Lord hath
set apart him that is godly for himself:
the Lord will hear when I call unto him.*
— *Psalms 4:3*

Psalm 4 shows confident prayer in action.
God's power is awesome, and the fear of
God helps to create the reverence with which
we pray to him for help.

*Is any sick among you?
let him call for the elders of the church;
and let them pray over him, anointing him
with oil in the name of the Lord.*
— James 5:14

Any illness is a pity, especially when a child is sick. We trust in the medicine and science God has made possible, but prayer also shows both God and our loved ones how invested we are.

*I*t may seem strange that
any men should dare to ask a just
God's assistance in wringing their bread
from the sweat of other men's faces,
but let us judge not, that we be not judged.
The prayers of both could not be answered.
That of neither has been answered fully.
The Almighty has His own purposes.
— *Abraham Lincoln*

*He that loveth not knoweth not God;
for God is love. In this was manifested
the love of God toward us, because that God
sent his only begotten Son into the world,
that we might live through him.*

— 1 John 4:8–9

I thank God through Jesus Christ our Lord.
— *Romans 7:25*

*S*ing and rejoice, O daughter of Zion:
for, lo, I come, and I will dwell in the midst
of thee, saith the Lord.
— *Zechariah 2:10*

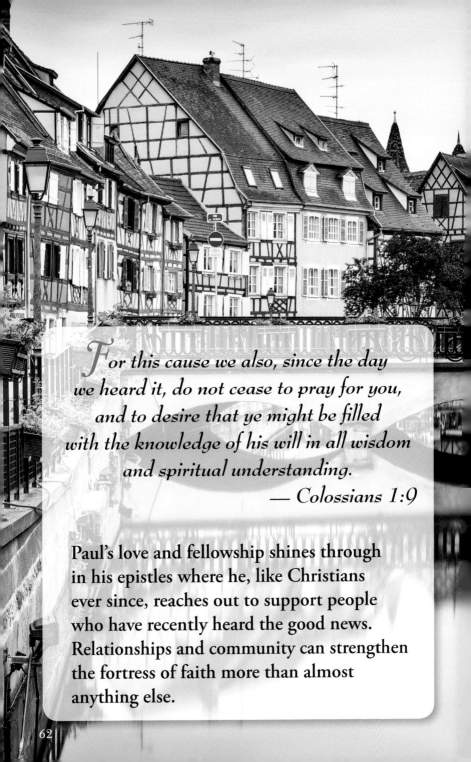

*For this cause we also, since the day
we heard it, do not cease to pray for you,
and to desire that ye might be filled
with the knowledge of his will in all wisdom
and spiritual understanding.*

— *Colossians 1:9*

Paul's love and fellowship shines through
in his epistles where he, like Christians
ever since, reaches out to support people
who have recently heard the good news.
Relationships and community can strengthen
the fortress of faith more than almost
anything else.

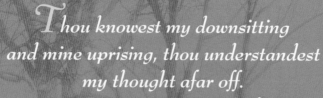

*Thou knowest my downsitting
and mine uprising, thou understandest
my thought afar off.*

— Psalms 139:2

*As every man hath received the gift,
even so minister the same one to another,
as good stewards of the manifold
grace of God.*

— 1 Peter 4:10

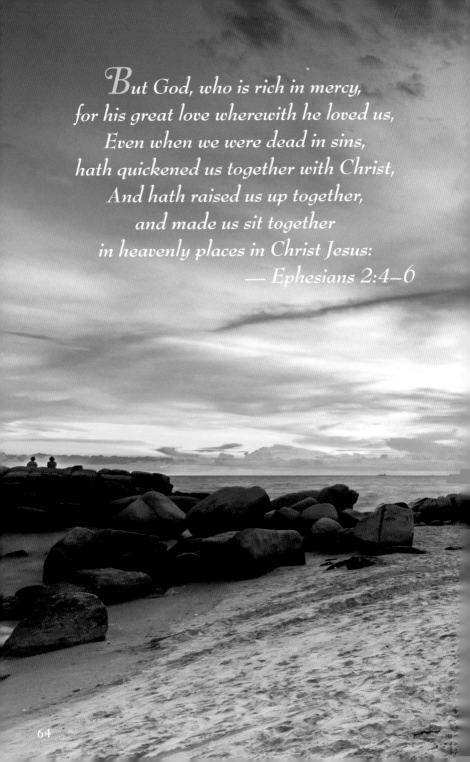

But God, who is rich in mercy,
for his great love wherewith he loved us,
Even when we were dead in sins,
hath quickened us together with Christ,
And hath raised us up together,
and made us sit together
in heavenly places in Christ Jesus:
— Ephesians 2:4–6

*I have blotted out, as a thick cloud,
thy transgressions, and, as a cloud, thy sins:
return unto me; for I have redeemed thee.*
                                  — Isaiah 44:22

Is there a burden or grudge you carry with
you? Imagine the same thick cloud
engulfing it and sweeping it out of your
mind. Ask God to help you forgive, rebuild,
and move on.

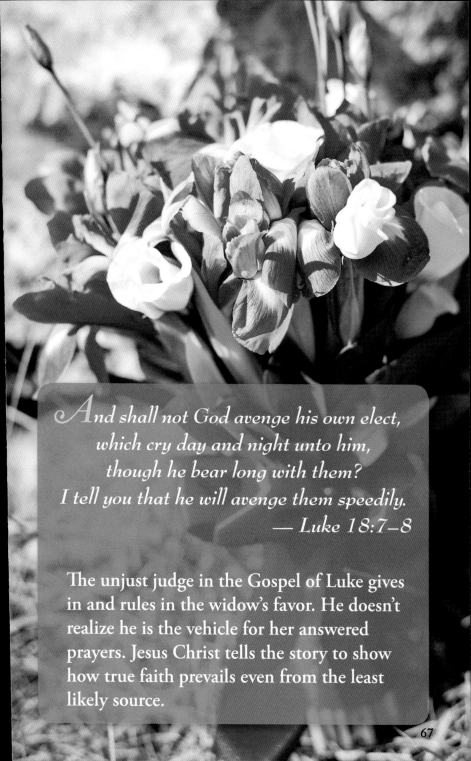

*And shall not God avenge his own elect,
which cry day and night unto him,
though he bear long with them?
I tell you that he will avenge them speedily.*
— Luke 18:7–8

The unjust judge in the Gospel of Luke gives
in and rules in the widow's favor. He doesn't
realize he is the vehicle for her answered
prayers. Jesus Christ tells the story to show
how true faith prevails even from the least
likely source.

*Behold, I will bring it health and cure,
and I will cure them, and will reveal
unto them the abundance of peace and truth.*
— *Jeremiah 33:6*

Inner peace and calm are vital to health.
Chronic stress weakens our immune systems
and impairs our bodies and minds. When
spiritual life seeks to replace illness and
doubt with "peace and truth," our minds
and bodies can thrive.

*But when ye pray, use not vain repetitions,
as the heathen do: for they think
that they shall be heard for their much
speaking. Be not ye therefore like unto them:
for your Father knoweth what things
ye have need of, before ye ask him.*

— Matthew 6:7–8

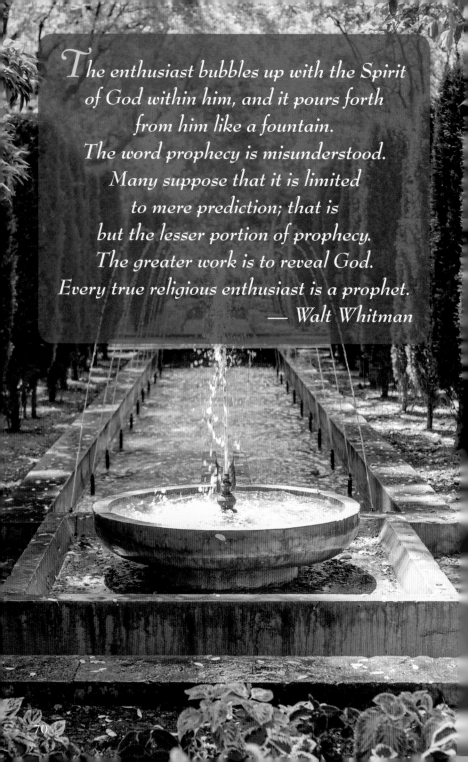

The enthusiast bubbles up with the Spirit
of God within him, and it pours forth
from him like a fountain.
The word prophecy is misunderstood.
Many suppose that it is limited
to mere prediction; that is
but the lesser portion of prophecy.
The greater work is to reveal God.
Every true religious enthusiast is a prophet.
— Walt Whitman

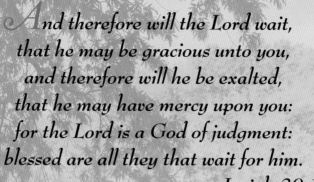

And therefore will the Lord wait,
that he may be gracious unto you,
and therefore will he be exalted,
that he may have mercy upon you:
for the Lord is a God of judgment:
blessed are all they that wait for him.
— Isaiah 30:18

Patience runs in both directions between us and God. Think about the relationships in your life: there must be people you wish were more patient, but are you also patient as you wait for them to learn?

God can't give His best till
we have given ours!
— Mary Slessor

Is there no balm in Gilead;
is there no physician there?
why then is not the health of the daughter
of my people recovered?
— Jeremiah 8:22

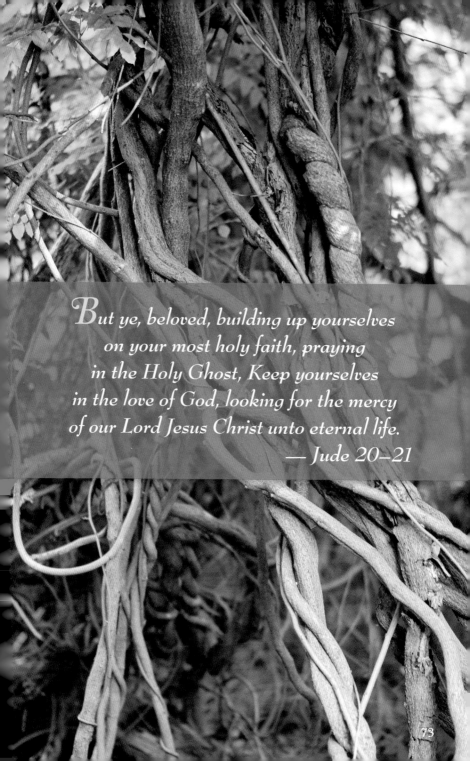

But ye, beloved, building up yourselves
on your most holy faith, praying
in the Holy Ghost, Keep yourselves
in the love of God, looking for the mercy
of our Lord Jesus Christ unto eternal life.

— Jude 20–21

*Cast yourself upon God, to do in you
what is impossible to man.*
— *Rev. Andrew Murray*

*If ye abide in me, and my words abide
in you, ye shall ask what ye will,
and it shall be done unto you.*
— *John 15:7*

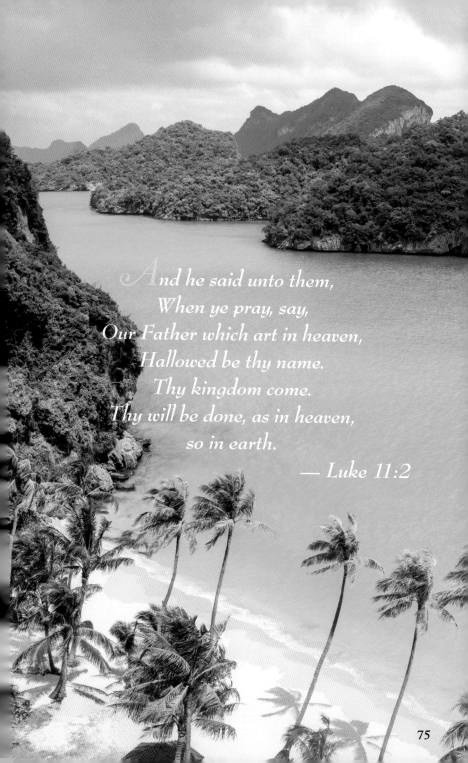

And he said unto them,
When ye pray, say,
Our Father which art in heaven,
Hallowed be thy name.
Thy kingdom come.
Thy will be done, as in heaven,
so in earth.

— Luke 11:2

To God I cried when troubles rose,
He heard me and subdued my foes,
He did my rising fears control,
And strength diffused through all my soul.
— Nancy Luce

As ye know how we exhorted
and comforted and charged
every one of you, as a father doth
his children, That ye would walk worthy
of God, who hath called you
unto his kingdom and glory.
For this cause also thank we God
without ceasing, because, when ye received
the word of God which ye heard of us,
ye received it not as the word of men,
but as it is in truth, the word of God,
which effectually worketh also
in you that believe.
— *1 Thessalonians 2:11–13*

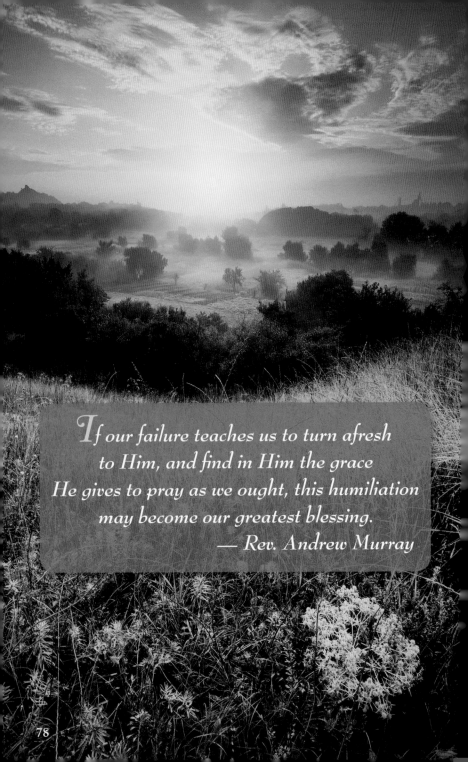

If our failure teaches us to turn afresh to Him, and find in Him the grace He gives to pray as we ought, this humiliation may become our greatest blessing.

— Rev. Andrew Murray

My God, my God,
why hast thou forsaken me?
why art thou so far from helping me,
and from the words
of my roaring?

— *Psalms 22:1*

It's tempting to bargain with God, which
tells us something interesting about human
nature: When we're convinced God has
chosen to ignore or forget us, we still beg for
his mercy, because we know he's listening.
His track record is perfect even when we
can't understand it for ourselves.

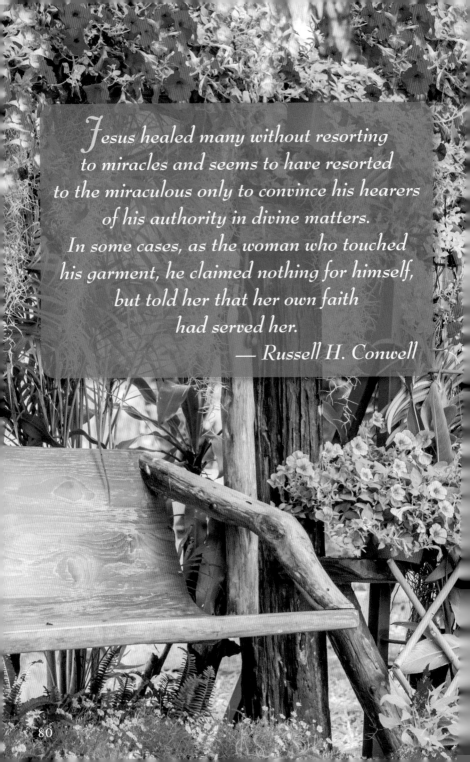

Jesus healed many without resorting
to miracles and seems to have resorted
to the miraculous only to convince his hearers
of his authority in divine matters.
In some cases, as the woman who touched
his garment, he claimed nothing for himself,
but told her that her own faith
had served her.

— Russell H. Conwell

*H*ear me when I call, O God
of my righteousness: thou hast enlarged me
when I was in distress; have mercy upon me,
and hear my prayer.

— Psalms 4:1

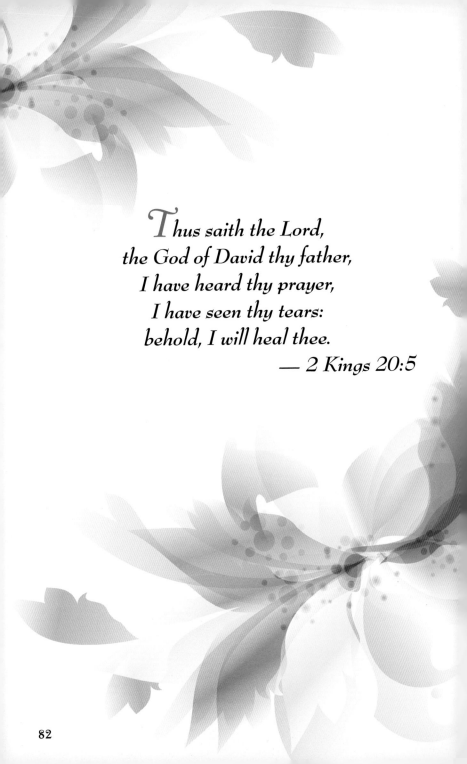

Thus saith the Lord,
the God of David thy father,
I have heard thy prayer,
I have seen thy tears:
behold, I will heal thee.

— *2 Kings 20:5*

*A*nd this is the confidence
that we have in him, that,
if we ask any thing according to his will,
he heareth us: And if we know
that he hear us, whatsoever we ask,
we know that we have the petitions
that we desired of him.

— 1 John 5:14–15

Humble yourselves in the sight of the Lord, and he shall lift you up.

— James 4:10

When thou vowest a vow unto God, defer not to pay it; for he hath no pleasure in fools: pay that which thou hast vowed.

— Ecclesiastes 5:4

*For the people shall dwell in Zion
at Jerusalem: thou shalt weep no more:
he will be very gracious unto thee
at the voice of thy cry; when he shall hear it,
he will answer thee.*

— Isaiah 30:19

When we're faced with obstacles, it's
tempting to keep trying anything and
everything in our power, but then we feel
hopeless if nothing works. We are never
hopeless in God's power.

*B*ut now, O Lord, thou art our father;
we are the clay, and thou our potter;
and we all are the work of thy hand.

— *Isaiah 64:8*

Have you worked with clay? It's flexible,
strong, and almost impossible to ruin. God
is the potter, but we, the clay, must hold our
shape and endure. If we're marred, the flaws
can be smoothed.

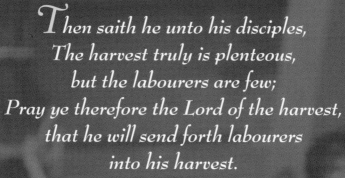

*T*hen saith he unto his disciples,
The harvest truly is plenteous,
but the labourers are few;
Pray ye therefore the Lord of the harvest,
that he will send forth labourers
into his harvest.

— Matthew 9:37–38

Here Jesus Christ calls for more religious "labourers" to help him preach to the growing crowds of believers. With too much to do and not enough help, our "harvests," whatever they may be, can also wither in the fields.

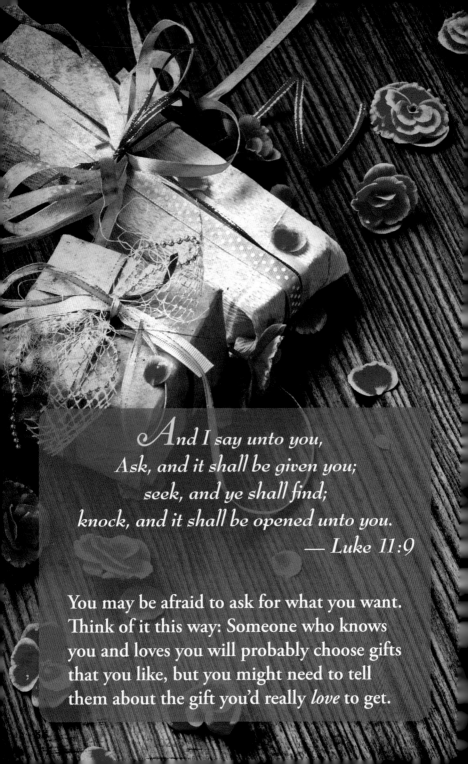

And I say unto you,
Ask, and it shall be given you;
seek, and ye shall find;
knock, and it shall be opened unto you.
— Luke 11:9

You may be afraid to ask for what you want.
Think of it this way: Someone who knows
you and loves you will probably choose gifts
that you like, but you might need to tell
them about the gift you'd really *love* to get.

Epaphras, who is one of you, a servant
of Christ, saluteth you, always labouring
fervently for you in prayers,
that ye may stand perfect and complete
in all the will of God.
— Colossians 4:12

All we really know about Epaphras is that
Paul shared Epaphras's kind words in a
handful of his epistles. It's lovely to think
about a network of very early believers who
cared so much for one another's beliefs and
salvation. They were loving and courageous
in a time when it endangered their lives.

$\mathcal{R}$ead the Psalms through,
making careful record of all the statements
of what the Lord was to the writers
of the Psalms. The list will surprise you.
Then on your knees go over them one by one,
with the prayer that Christ may be to you
what he was to David and the others.

— Rosalind Goforth

*T*hou compassest my path
and my lying down,
and art acquainted with all my ways.
For there is not a word in my tongue,
but, lo, O Lord, thou knowest it altogether.
— *Psalms 139:3–4*

*A*nd it came to pass in those days,
that he went out into a mountain to pray,
and continued all night in prayer to God.

— *Luke 6:12*

Solitude can be the best spiritual medium.
People have always been moved to pray by
the beauty and sheer scale of the outdoors,
surrounded by God's creation.

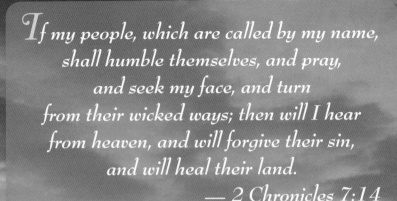

*If my people, which are called by my name,
shall humble themselves, and pray,
and seek my face, and turn
from their wicked ways; then will I hear
from heaven, and will forgive their sin,
and will heal their land.*

— 2 Chronicles 7:14

We pray in desperate or troubling times, and these prayers can include promises to give up a bad habit or behavior. Why wait for a trial in order to make a pledge to God?

*I cried unto him with my mouth,
and he was extolled with my tongue.*

— Psalms 66:17

*And when ye stand praying, forgive,
if ye have ought against any:
that your Father also which is in heaven
may forgive you your trespasses.*

— Mark 11:25

*P*rayer has been hedged about
with too many man-made rules.
I am convinced that God has intended prayer
to be as simple and natural, and as constant
a part of our spiritual life, as the intercourse
between a child and his parent in the home.
— Rosalind Goforth

*In the day of my trouble I sought the Lord:
my sore ran in the night, and ceased not:
my soul refused to be comforted.*

— Psalms 77:2

The darker Psalms serve an important purpose by giving us an outlet when our own souls refuse to be comforted. We want to cry or scream in frustration until we feel ready to return to God.

*Let your conversation be
without covetousness;
and be content with such things as ye have:
for he hath said, I will never leave thee,
nor forsake thee.*

— Hebrews 13:5

Like an ersatz wedding invitation, God's presence is present enough. Think about an item you wish you had — a newer car, a bigger house — and imagine all the better "things unseen" that you have instead.

*B*eloved child of God!
you know by experience how little
an intellectual apprehension
of truth has profited you.
Beseech God to reveal Himself to you.
— Rev. Andrew Murray

The idea is foolishly unrighteous
which looks upon the arrangement
of Providence as a slot machine
into which the pretended worshiper
may put a copper penny
and draw out a gold dollar.
As gold must be given for gold,
so love must be given for love.
— Russell H. Conwell

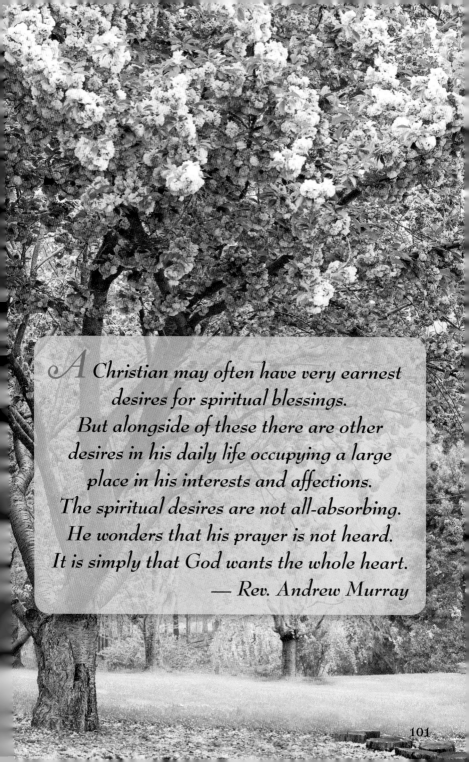

A Christian may often have very earnest
desires for spiritual blessings.
But alongside of these there are other
desires in his daily life occupying a large
place in his interests and affections.
The spiritual desires are not all-absorbing.
He wonders that his prayer is not heard.
It is simply that God wants the whole heart.
— Rev. Andrew Murray

*F*or verily I say unto you,
That whosoever shall say
unto this mountain, Be thou removed,
and be thou cast into the sea;
and shall not doubt in his heart,
but shall believe that those things
which he saith shall come to pass;
he shall have whatsoever he saith.

— Mark 11:23

*Righteous art thou, O Lord,
when I plead with thee.*
— Jeremiah 12:1

*Let us stir up the slumbering gift
that is lying unused, and seek to gather
and train and band together
as many as we can.*
— Rev. Andrew Murray

Help me, O Lord my God:
O save me according to thy mercy:
That they may know that this is thy hand;
that thou, Lord, hast done it.
                              — Psalms 109:26–27

Some people say adult life is like high school repeated, with all the cliques, scheming, and backstabbing you could ask for. But our relationship with God should make us bigger and better. Living well is the best resolution, as they say.

*O*ne day, two boys came in, and we had everything to clothe them except a jacket for one of them. The matron, a very godly woman, said, "We must just pray that God will send what is needed," and we prayed that He would. That night a large [parcel] of clothing came, and in it was a jacket that fitted the boy as if it had been made for him. That was a small thing, of course, but if you don't see God in the gift of a pair of stockings you won't see Him in a gift of $10,000.

— *William Quarrier*

It is not a question of what you can do;
it is the question of whether you now,
with your whole heart, turn to give God
His due, and give yourself to let His will
and grace have their way with you.
— Rev. Andrew Murray

It can never be wrong to ask
to be made right.
— *Charles Kingsley*

*B*ut we will give ourselves continually
to prayer, and to the ministry of the word.
— *Acts 6:4*

For the promise is unto you,
and to your children,
and to all that are afar off,
even as many as the Lord our God shall call.
— Acts 2:39

Christians cover the world, as "afar off" as anyone could get. But think about the spiritual distance that grows between us and God when we're stretched too thin or simply don't want to reach for him. How can we narrow that gap?

I the Lord have spoken it, and I will do it.
— *Ezekiel 36:36*

If only we could be as consistent as God is with our own promises of punishments or rewards. Draw strength from his example!

*T*he father who would not give a stone
to his child who asked for bread
would not give a stone to his starving child
who asked for a stone.
— *Russell H. Conwell*

111

*A*nd it shall be to me a name of joy,
a praise and an honour before all the nations
of the earth, which shall hear all the good
that I do unto them: and they shall fear
and tremble for all the goodness and
for all the prosperity that I procure unto it.

— Jeremiah 33:9

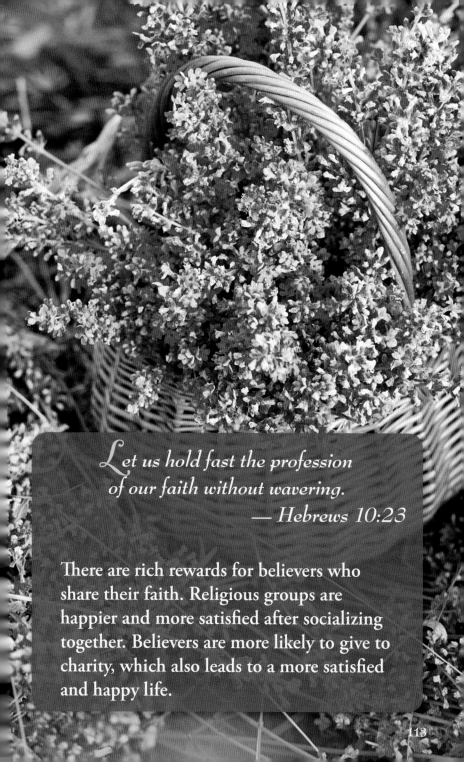

*Let us hold fast the profession
of our faith without wavering.*
— *Hebrews 10:23*

There are rich rewards for believers who share their faith. Religious groups are happier and more satisfied after socializing together. Believers are more likely to give to charity, which also leads to a more satisfied and happy life.

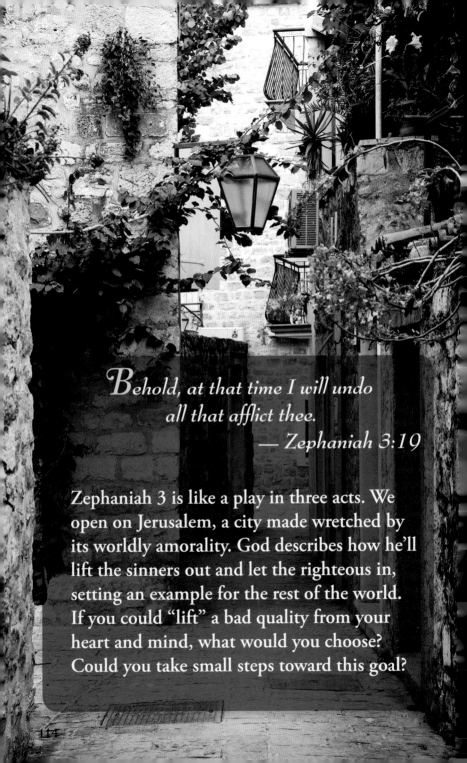

*Behold, at that time I will undo
all that afflict thee.*
— *Zephaniah 3:19*

Zephaniah 3 is like a play in three acts. We open on Jerusalem, a city made wretched by its worldly amorality. God describes how he'll lift the sinners out and let the righteous in, setting an example for the rest of the world. If you could "lift" a bad quality from your heart and mind, what would you choose? Could you take small steps toward this goal?

Looking unto Jesus the author and finisher of our faith; who for the joy that was set before him endured the cross, despising the shame, and is set down at the right hand of the throne of God.

— Hebrews 12:2

Reflect on the idea of a "finisher," like the keystone in an archway. Without the keystone, the arch collapses, no matter how the other stones are arranged.

Trusteth in God, and continueth in supplications and prayers night and day.
— *1 Timothy 5:5*

Throughout the Bible we see these exhortations to both faith and works. In 1 Timothy 5 we learn to expect this of our fellow believers and to let social support bring us all closer to God. Who bolsters your faith?

I am the vine, ye are the branches:
He that abideth in me, and I in him,
the same bringeth forth much fruit:
for without me ye can do nothing.
— John 15:5

With God, you have everything — without God, you have nothing. The contrast is stark and effective. All good things must come through a relationship with God. If they don't, then they're not truly good — buyer beware.

*S*et your affection on things above,
not on things on the earth.
— Colossians 3:2

*I*s any among you afflicted? let him pray.
Is any merry? let him sing psalms.
— James 5:13

Ah Lord God! behold, thou hast made the heaven and the earth by thy great power and stretched out arm, and there is nothing too hard for thee.
— *Jeremiah 32:17*

Jeremiah is a role model for how to pray in a challenging situation. He knows that God is all powerful and can't make a "bad" decision, but he is also struggling to understand the situation from his earthly perspective. Jeremiah is reverent as he opens his heart to God, and he receives a helpful, supportive answer.

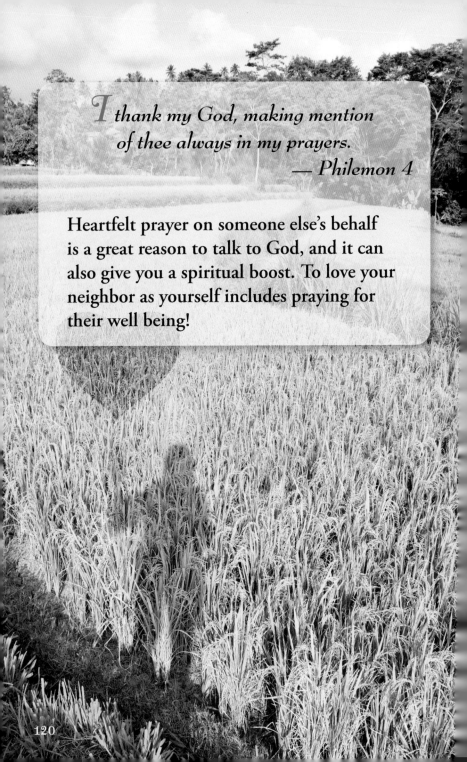

I thank my God, making mention of thee always in my prayers.

— *Philemon 4*

Heartfelt prayer on someone else's behalf is a great reason to talk to God, and it can also give you a spiritual boost. To love your neighbor as yourself includes praying for their well being!

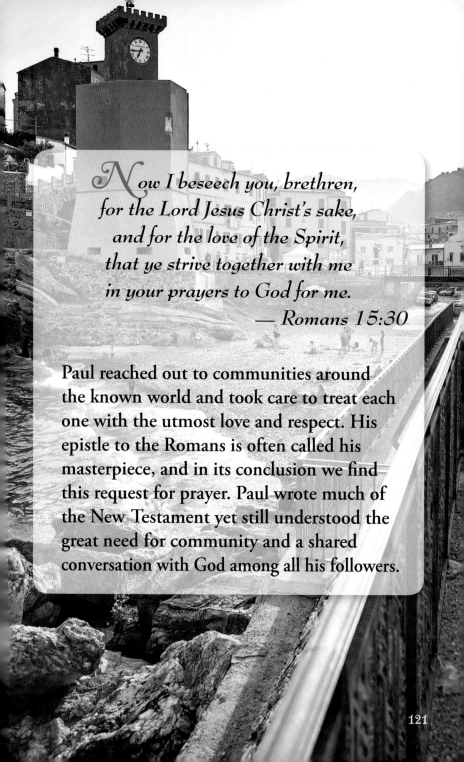

*$\mathcal{N}$ow I beseech you, brethren,
for the Lord Jesus Christ's sake,
and for the love of the Spirit,
that ye strive together with me
in your prayers to God for me.*
— *Romans 15:30*

Paul reached out to communities around the known world and took care to treat each one with the utmost love and respect. His epistle to the Romans is often called his masterpiece, and in its conclusion we find this request for prayer. Paul wrote much of the New Testament yet still understood the great need for community and a shared conversation with God among all his followers.

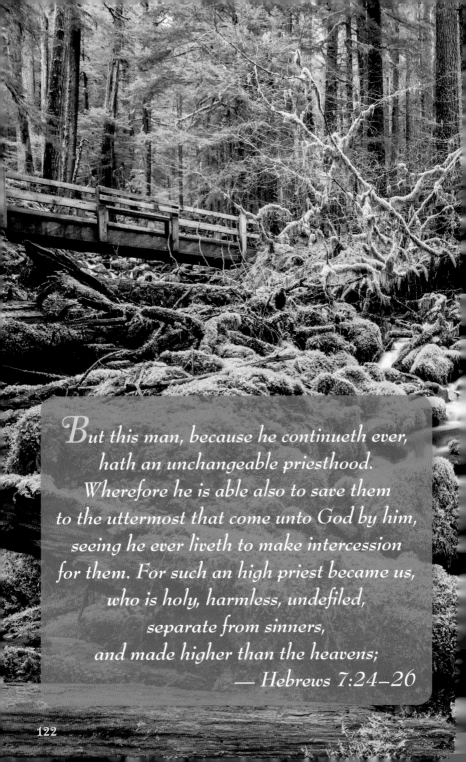

*But this man, because he continueth ever,
hath an unchangeable priesthood.
Wherefore he is able also to save them
to the uttermost that come unto God by him,
seeing he ever liveth to make intercession
for them. For such an high priest became us,
who is holy, harmless, undefiled,
separate from sinners,
and made higher than the heavens;*
— Hebrews 7:24–26

*O Lord, I have heard thy speech,
and was afraid: O Lord, revive thy work
in the midst of the years, in the midst
of the years make known;
in wrath remember mercy.*
— *Habakkuk 3:2*

God can do anything, so Habakkuk's request for mercy is a hopeful paean instead of the difficult near-contradiction it presents to us. But to be merciful is a great blessing to both giver and receiver, a challenge worth accepting.

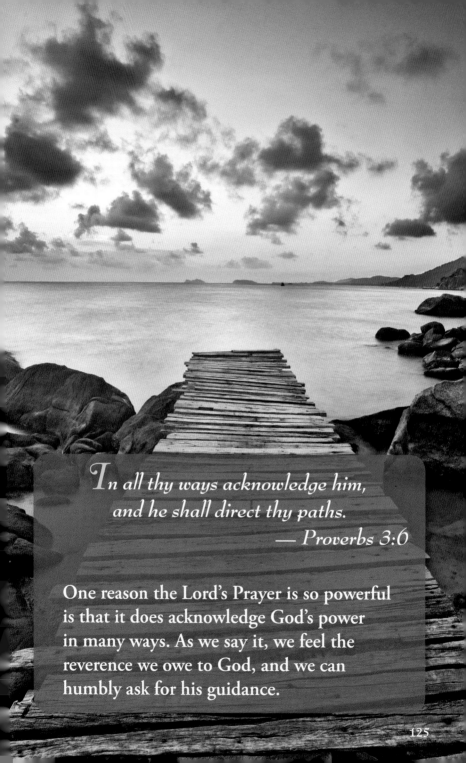

*In all thy ways acknowledge him,
and he shall direct thy paths.*
— *Proverbs 3:6*

One reason the Lord's Prayer is so powerful is that it does acknowledge God's power in many ways. As we say it, we feel the reverence we owe to God, and we can humbly ask for his guidance.

And Jesus stood,
and commanded him
to be brought unto him:
and when he was come near,
he asked him, Saying,
What wilt thou that I shall do unto thee?
And he said, Lord,
that I may receive my sight.

— *Luke 18:40–41*

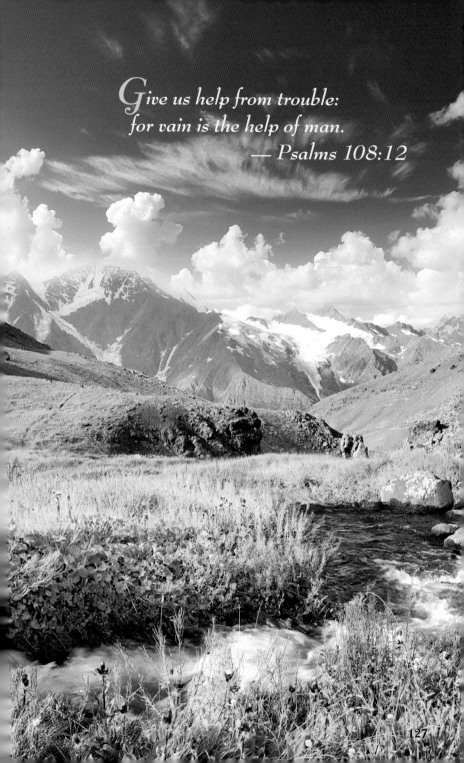

Give us help from trouble:
for vain is the help of man.
— Psalms 108:12

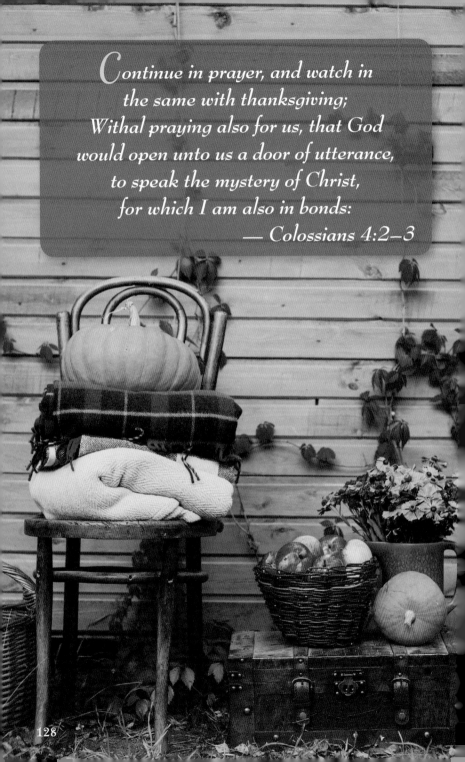

Continue in prayer, and watch in
the same with thanksgiving;
Withal praying also for us, that God
would open unto us a door of utterance,
to speak the mystery of Christ,
for which I am also in bonds:
— Colossians 4:2–3

*S*it thou on my right hand,
Until I make thy foes thy footstool.
— *Acts 2:34–35*

*B*lessed be God, which hath not turned
away my prayer, nor his mercy from me.
— *Psalms 66:20*

$\mathcal{T}$hus saith the Lord,
In an acceptable time have I heard thee,
and in a day of salvation have I helped thee:
and I will preserve thee,
and give thee for a covenant of the people,
to establish the earth.

— *Isaiah 49:8*

If ye shall ask any thing in my name,
I will do it.

— *John 14:14*

I have declared my ways,
and thou heardest me:
teach me thy statutes.
— Psalms 119:26

*H*ear, O heavens, and give ear, O earth:
for the Lord hath spoken,
I have nourished and brought up children,
and they have rebelled against me.
— Isaiah 1:2

*That Christ may dwell in your hearts
by faith; that ye, being rooted and grounded
in love, May be able to comprehend
with all saints what is the breadth,
and length, and depth, and height;
And to know the love of Christ,
which passeth knowledge, that ye might be
filled with all the fulness of God.*

— Ephesians 3:17–19

Let every physician, before he begins
his treatment, offer up a secret prayer
for the sick person, and implore
the heavenly Father, the Physician
and Balm-giver of all mankind, to prosper
the work he is entering upon, and to save
himself and his patient from failure.

— P. W. Joyce

If I regard iniquity in my heart,
the Lord will not hear me.
— *Psalms 66:18*

When you take time to "consider your ways," do you find scraps of envy or other sins that you can release from your mind? Could a loved one or friend talk them out with you? Could you share them with God and ask for his support?

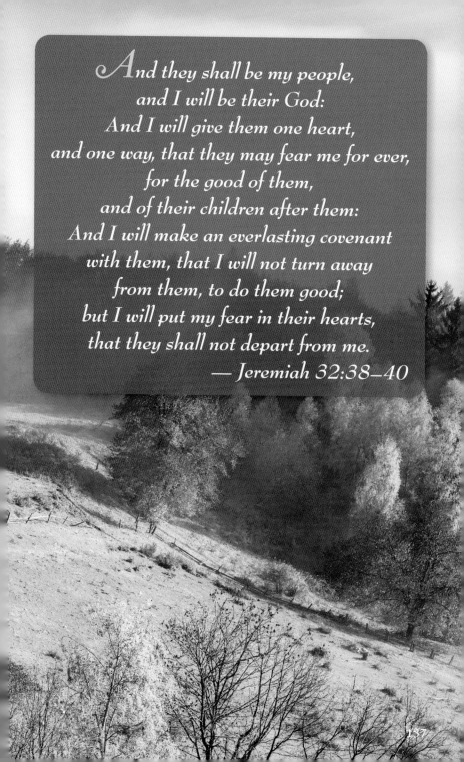

And they shall be my people,
and I will be their God:
And I will give them one heart,
and one way, that they may fear me for ever,
for the good of them,
and of their children after them:
And I will make an everlasting covenant
with them, that I will not turn away
from them, to do them good;
but I will put my fear in their hearts,
that they shall not depart from me.
— Jeremiah 32:38–40

*T*ake courage. The burden and the agony,
the triumph and the victory are all His.
Learn from Him, yield to His Spirit in you,
to know how to pray.

— Rev. Andrew Murray

*F*or whosoever shall call upon the name
of the Lord shall be saved.

— *Romans 10:13*

*B*etter is it that thou shouldest not vow,
than that thou shouldest vow and not pay.

— *Ecclesiastes 5:5*

*And the prayer of faith shall save the sick,
and the Lord shall raise him up;
and if he have committed sins,
they shall be forgiven him.*

— James 5:15

John Donne wrote a series of prayers as
he recovered from a serious illness, each
expressing his frustration and devotion
to God. Many of his most famous lines are
from these laments and devotions.

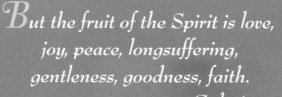

But the fruit of the Spirit is love, joy, peace, longsuffering, gentleness, goodness, faith.
— *Galatians 5:22*

"Longsuffering" really sneaks in among the fun-sounding qualities and puts a damper on things. But longsuffering can be reframed as tenacity or endurance: the strength to always keep going, to keep walking in faith, despite the obstacles and grind of daily life. The obstacles themselves will vary, but we know there will always be obstacles.

And when thou prayest,
thou shalt not be as the hypocrites are:
for they love to pray standing
in the synagogues and in the corners
of the streets, that they may be seen of men.

— Matthew 6:5

And let us consider one another
to provoke unto love and to good works.
— *Hebrews 10:24*

Studies show that good works like charity
are "contagious" in social groups. People
who know their friends or neighbors are
giving are more likely to give themselves.
We may feel more comfortable volunteering
if a friend or loved one will be there with us.
In turn, these shared acts help to foster our
love for neighbors and community.

So in all things, that which God has
given me intelligence and power to do,
in avoiding evil or securing good,
I am under direct command from him to do,
always depending upon His blessing
to secure the needed result.
A true faith in God will be made manifest
by careful obedience to known commands.
An intelligent faith can never allow
dependence upon means used to take the
place of dependence upon the living God,

— D. W. Whittle

For what thanks can we render to God again for you, for all the joy wherewith we joy for your sakes before our God; Night and day praying exceedingly that we might see your face, and might perfect that which is lacking in your faith?
— 1 Thessalonians 3:9–10

*Yea, thou castest off fear,
and restrainest prayer before God.*
— Job 15:4

*Submit yourselves therefore to God.
Resist the devil, and he will flee from you.*
— James 4:7

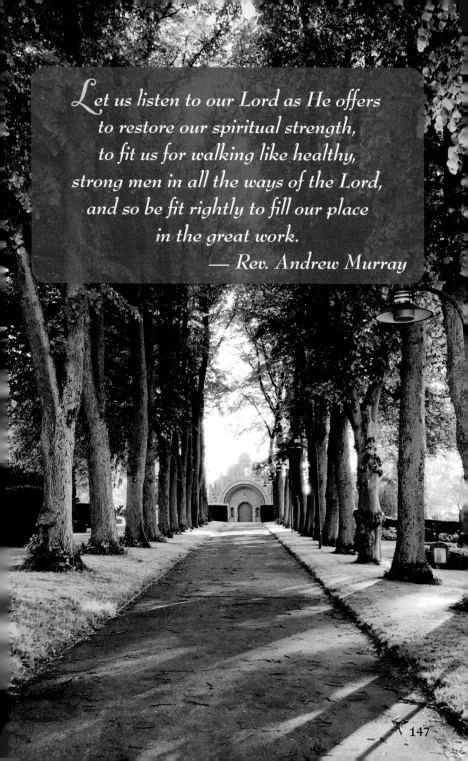

Let us listen to our Lord as He offers
to restore our spiritual strength,
to fit us for walking like healthy,
strong men in all the ways of the Lord,
and so be fit rightly to fill our place
in the great work.

— Rev. Andrew Murray

That thy beloved may be delivered:
save with thy right hand, and answer me.
— *Psalms 108:6*

When we're waiting to make progress —
a job offer, medical test, important phone
call — all we can think about is the
missing piece of information. Waiting
to hear from God can feel the same way.
We want his blessing or simply to see his
work in our lives, and we must be patient.

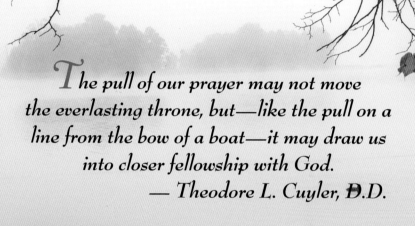

The pull of our prayer may not move
the everlasting throne, but—like the pull on a
line from the bow of a boat—it may draw us
into closer fellowship with God.
— Theodore L. Cuyler, D.D.

*O*pen thou mine eyes, that I may
behold wondrous things out of thy law.
— *Psalms 119:18*

O give thanks unto the Lord, for he is good:
for his mercy endureth for ever.
— *Psalms 107:1*

Wherefore seeing we also are compassed about with so great a cloud of witnesses, let us lay aside every weight, and the sin which doth so easily beset us, and let us run with patience the race that is set before us

— Hebrews 12:1

The trusting believer in prayer rests in God in a peaceful condition of soul.

— Russell H. Conwell

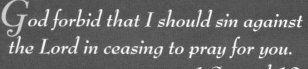

God forbid that I should sin against the Lord in ceasing to pray for you.
— *1 Samuel 12:23*

Samuel's comment can seem like a nicety as he says goodbye to the Israelites, but his fear of God is very real. The Israelites demanded a king; God agreed but made sure they knew, in words and with thunder, that they'd been sinful to question God. Samuel must pray for them both as a believer himself and as a prophet.

*A*nd Cornelius said, Four days ago
I was fasting until this hour;
and at the ninth hour I prayed in my house,
and, behold, a man stood before me
in bright clothing, And said, Cornelius,
thy prayer is heard, and thine alms are had
in remembrance in the sight of God.
— *Acts 10:30–31*

For thine eyes are open upon all the ways of the sons of men: to give every one according to his ways, and according to the fruit of his doings.

— *Jeremiah 32:19*

Think of someone you respect and admire, and imagine their "ways and doings" listed alongside your own. How do the lists compare and contrast? There is probably an opportunity to improve hiding in your daily routine.

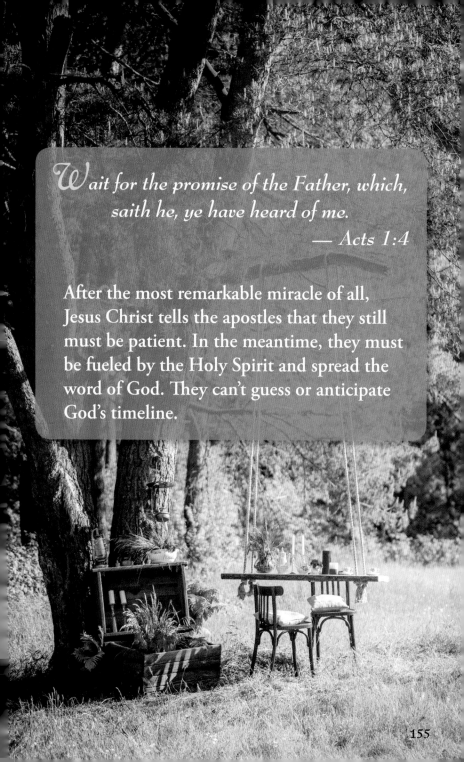

Wait for the promise of the Father, which, saith he, ye have heard of me.

— *Acts 1:4*

After the most remarkable miracle of all, Jesus Christ tells the apostles that they still must be patient. In the meantime, they must be fueled by the Holy Spirit and spread the word of God. They can't guess or anticipate God's timeline.

By him therefore let us offer the sacrifice
of praise to God continually, that is,
the fruit of our lips giving thanks to his name.
But to do good and to communicate
forget not: for with such sacrifices
God is well pleased.
— Hebrews 13:15–16

*T*hus saith the Lord of hosts;
Consider your ways.
— *Haggai 1:7*

*F*ollow peace with all men, and holiness,
without which no man shall see the Lord.
— *Hebrews 12:14*

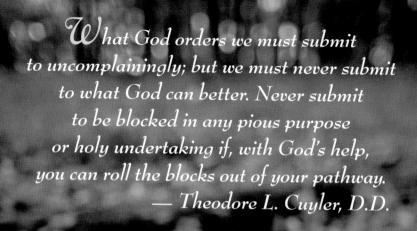

*W*hat God orders we must submit
to uncomplainingly; but we must never submit
to what God can better. Never submit
to be blocked in any pious purpose
or holy undertaking if, with God's help,
you can roll the blocks out of your pathway.
— *Theodore L. Cuyler, D.D.*

*Or let him take hold of my strength,
that he may make peace with me.*

— Isaiah 27:5

God speaks of Israel as a vine to be nurtured, and a vine must have support in order to climb and thrive. We're surrounded by these outposts of God, these potential sources of strength, toward which we can reach and grow.

Brethren, my heart's desire and prayer to God for Israel is, that they might be saved.
— *Romans 10:1*

Paul explains in careful detail how all people are still near to God and can easily take the final step toward Jesus Christ. He wades deep into theology but never loses sight of his personal relationship with God and his fellow man. He remembers his past as an unbeliever and has compassion.

Behold, the Lord's hand is not shortened,
that it cannot save; neither his ear heavy,
that it cannot hear: But your iniquities
have separated between you and your God,
and your sins have hid his face from you,
that he will not hear.

— Isaiah 59:1–2

Woe to the rebellious children,
saith the Lord, that take counsel,
but not of me.

— Isaiah 30:1

When we need advice, it can be tempting to comparison shop, like a child asking a fortune-telling toy the same question over and over. Often our gut instinct tells us the right answer, informed by our relationship with God, our morals, and our values.

*L*et us draw near with a true heart
in full assurance of faith, having our hearts
sprinkled from an evil conscience,
and our bodies washed with pure water.
— *Hebrews 10:22*

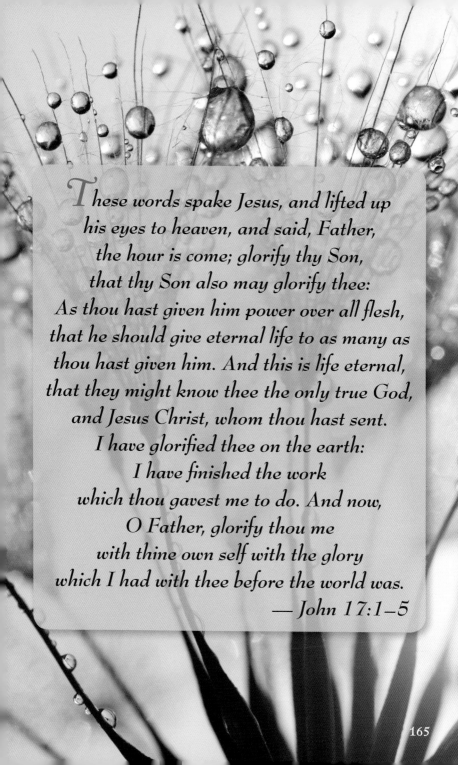

*These words spake Jesus, and lifted up
his eyes to heaven, and said, Father,
the hour is come; glorify thy Son,
that thy Son also may glorify thee:
As thou hast given him power over all flesh,
that he should give eternal life to as many as
thou hast given him. And this is life eternal,
that they might know thee the only true God,
and Jesus Christ, whom thou hast sent.
I have glorified thee on the earth:
I have finished the work
which thou gavest me to do. And now,
O Father, glorify thou me
with thine own self with the glory
which I had with thee before the world was.
— John 17:1–5*

165

*W*herefore gird up the loins of your mind,
be sober, and hope to the end for the grace
that is to be brought unto you
at the revelation of Jesus Christ;
As obedient children, not fashioning
yourselves according to the former lusts
in your ignorance: But as he which hath
called you is holy, so be ye holy in all manner
of conversation; Because it is written,
Be ye holy; for I am holy.
— 1 Peter 1:13–16

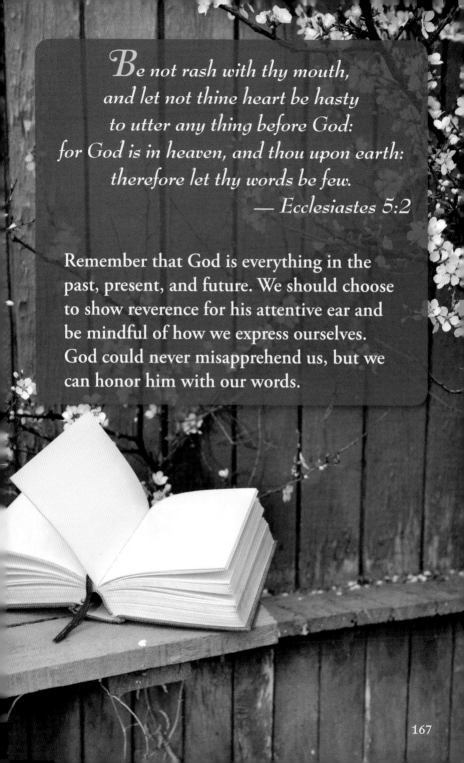

*Be not rash with thy mouth,
and let not thine heart be hasty
to utter any thing before God:
for God is in heaven, and thou upon earth:
therefore let thy words be few.*
— Ecclesiastes 5:2

Remember that God is everything in the past, present, and future. We should choose to show reverence for his attentive ear and be mindful of how we express ourselves. God could never misapprehend us, but we can honor him with our words.

167

*Trust in the Lord with all thine heart;
and lean not unto thine own understanding.*

— Proverbs 3:5

Ask ye of the Lord rain in the time
of the latter rain; so the Lord shall make
bright clouds, and give them showers of rain,
to every one grass in the field.
— Zechariah 10:1

169

I cried with my whole heart;
hear me, O Lord:
I will keep thy statutes.
— Psalms 119:145

And for those who know not Christ?
What will happen to them we know not:
but this we know, that they are his sheep,
lost sheep though they may be;
and that we are bound to pray,
that he would bring them home to his flock.
— Charles Kingsley

*But verily God hath heard me;
he hath attended to the voice of my prayer.*
— Psalms 66:19

*For I have given you an example,
that ye should do as I have done to you.*
— John 13:15

*And so it may come to pass
in later life that our specific petitions
for this or that thing may grow fewer.
To put it another way—the petitions are
fewer because the prayer is deeper and truer.
— W. Boyd Carpenter, D.D.*

Turn ye unto me, saith the Lord of hosts, and I will turn unto you.

— *Zechariah 1:3*

Is an opportunity waiting for you to "put yourself out there"? A setback or bad decision can lead us to hesitate before God, as though he only loves us when our behavior is flawless.

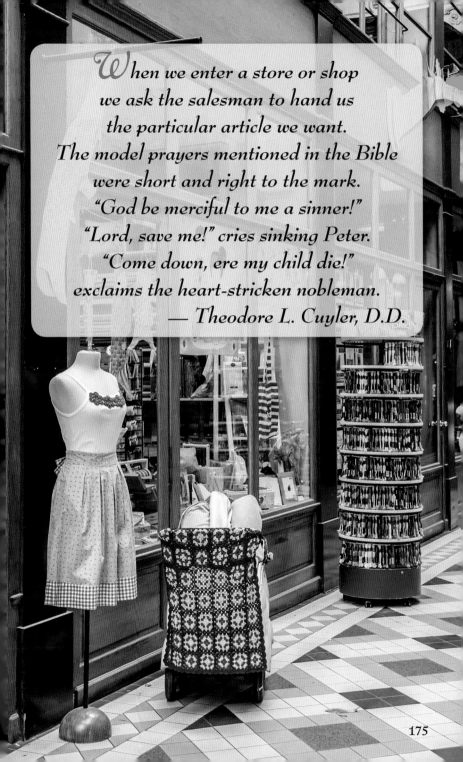

*W*hen we enter a store or shop
we ask the salesman to hand us
the particular article we want.
The model prayers mentioned in the Bible
were short and right to the mark.
"God be merciful to me a sinner!"
"Lord, save me!" cries sinking Peter.
"Come down, ere my child die!"
exclaims the heart-stricken nobleman.
— Theodore L. Cuyler, D.D.

O my God, I cry in the day time,
but thou hearest not;
and in the night season,
and am not silent.

— Psalms 22:2

This lament is poignant, but its message is uplifting: the psalmist wonders if God is listening yet prays to God about it. We relate to the psalmist's feelings and are inspired by his optimism.

*H*er priests have violated my law,
and have profaned mine holy things:
they have put no difference between the holy
and profane, neither have they shewed
difference between the unclean and the clean,
and have hid their eyes from my sabbaths,
and I am profaned among them.

— *Ezekiel 22:26*

We give thanks to God always for you all, making mention of you in our prayers.

— 1 Thessalonians 1:2

Expressing gratitude is a simple way to feel more connected: to our loved ones, to our daily lives, and to God. Taking time to pray for your own "you all" is good for everyone involved.

*A*nd without controversy great
is the mystery of godliness:
God was manifest in the flesh,
justified in the Spirit, seen of angels,
preached unto the Gentiles, believed on
in the world, received up into glory.
— 1 Timothy 3:16

*T*hese all continued with one accord in prayer and supplication.

— *Acts 1:14*

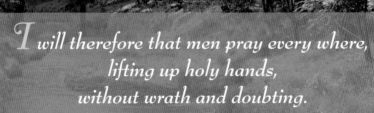

I will therefore that men pray every where,
lifting up holy hands,
without wrath and doubting.

— *1 Timothy 2:8*

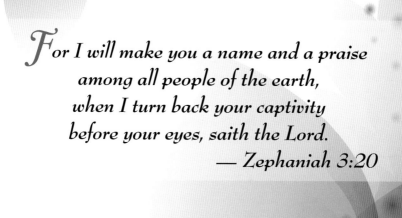

*For I will make you a name and a praise
among all people of the earth,
when I turn back your captivity
before your eyes, saith the Lord.*
                    — Zephaniah 3:20

Grace be to you, and peace,
from God our Father,
and from the Lord Jesus Christ.
— Ephesians 1:2

All the epistles have beautiful greetings,
specific to each audience. The Ephesians
lived in a blended society, and Paul urges
them to treat one another with deference
and respect — perhaps hinted at here by his
mention of peace. His message to coexist in
the Lord is timeless.

*Thou hast beset me behind and before,
and laid thine hand upon me.
Such knowledge is too wonderful for me;
it is high, I cannot attain unto it.*

— Psalms 139:5–6

"Amazing Grace" compares finding God
to moving from blindness to sight, but the
distance is just as great from our own sight
to God's.

Yet I will rejoice in the Lord,
I will joy in the God of my salvation.
— Habakkuk 3:18

I will greatly praise the Lord with my mouth;
yea, I will praise him among the multitude.
— Psalms 109:30

*For neither at any time used
we flattering words, as ye know,
nor a cloke of covetousness; God is witness:
Nor of men sought we glory, neither of you,
nor yet of others, when we might have been
burdensome, as the apostles of Christ.*
— 1 Thessalonians 2:5–6

When I was a young woman I prayed for three years that God would grant me a certain petition. Sometimes I pleaded for this as for life itself, so intensely did I want it. Then God showed me very clearly that I was praying against his will. I resigned my will to his in the matter, and a few months later God gave what was infinitely better.

— Rosalind Goforth

Ye have wearied the Lord with your words.
Yet ye say, Wherein have we wearied him?
— *Malachi 2:17*

From scripture we learn to choose our words
carefully when we talk to God, and to do
this we have to be open to critique, even if
it's only from ourselves.

Two lovers, separated far and praying long for each other, is an exhibition of the truest, sweetest love. It is, also, the best test of God's disposition to heed the requests of his children. No prayer for another can be felt to be effective which is not inspired more or less by real love.

— Russell H. Conwell

*G*od does not deal with all alike,
either in His gifts of faith
or in those of experience.
We differ also in the use we make of His gifts.
— W. Boyd Carpenter, D.D.

With my whole heart have I sought thee:
O let me not wander
from thy commandments.
— Psalms 119:10

[Justice and honesty] are God's gift, and not
any natural product of our own hearts:
and for that very reason we can and must
keep them alive in us by prayer.
— *Charles Kingsley*

*It is good for me that I have been afflicted;
that I might learn thy statutes.*
— Psalms 119:71

There's a paradox in learning from our
mistakes, because we have to be able to see
and understand them as mistakes in order to
glean the lesson. And it's always as humbling
as it was the first time.

There were times when my faith was
severely tested, and I fear too often
I did not stand the test;
but oh, how patient God is with us
in our human weakness.

— Rosalind Goforth

*T*hou hast given him his heart's desire, and hast not withholden the request of his lips.
— *Psalms 21:2*

*M*y little children, let us not love in word, neither in tongue; but in deed and in truth.
— *1 John 3:18*

*When Jesus saw him lie, and knew that
he had been now a long time in that case,
he saith unto him, Wilt thou be made whole?
The impotent man answered him, Sir,
I have no man, when the water is troubled,
to put me into the pool: but while I am
coming, another steppeth down before me.
Jesus saith unto him, Rise, take up
thy bed, and walk. And immediately
the man was made whole,
and took up his bed, and walked.*

— *John 5:6–9*

*S*o then they that are in the flesh cannot please God. But ye are not in the flesh, but in the Spirit, if so be that the Spirit of God dwell in you. Now if any man have not the Spirit of Christ, he is none of his. And if Christ be in you, the body is dead because of sin; but the Spirit is life because of righteousness.

— Romans 8:8–10

*We can only obtain God's best
by fitness of receiving power.
Without receivers fitted and kept
in order the air may tingle
and thrill with the message, but it will not
reach my spirit and consciousness.*

— *Mary Slessor*

*And the Lord appeared to Solomon
by night, and said unto him,
I have heard thy prayer.*
— *2 Chronicles 7:12*

King Solomon built a temple and prayed
for God to bless it with his presence. God
chose to favor the temple as a place for
worship, putting a sacred space in the center
of a group of believers. Chances are good
that your church is still part of the social
backbone of your community.

*But the end of all things is at hand:
be ye therefore sober, and watch unto prayer.
And above all things have fervent charity
among yourselves: for charity shall cover
the multitude of sins. Use hospitality one
to another without grudging.*
— 1 Peter 4:7–9

*Follow righteousness, faith, charity, peace,
with them that call on the Lord
out of a pure heart.*
— *2 Timothy 2:22*

*F*or I will pour water
upon him that is thirsty,
and floods upon the dry ground:
I will pour my spirit upon thy seed,
and my blessing upon thine offspring.

— Isaiah 44:3

201

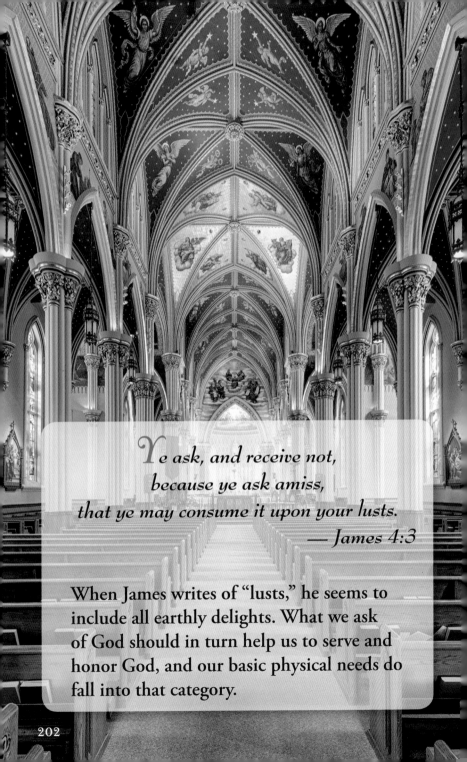

*Y*e ask, and receive not,
because ye ask amiss,
that ye may consume it upon your lusts.

— *James 4:3*

When James writes of "lusts," he seems to
include all earthly delights. What we ask
of God should in turn help us to serve and
honor God, and our basic physical needs do
fall into that category.

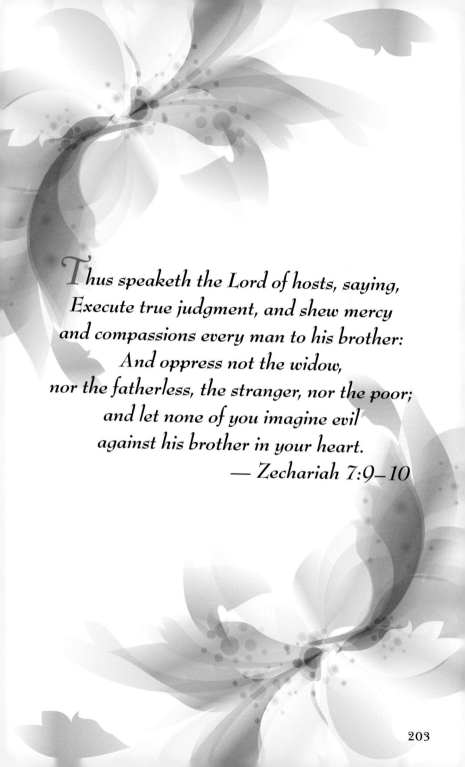

*T*hus speaketh the Lord of hosts, saying,
Execute true judgment, and shew mercy
and compassions every man to his brother:
And oppress not the widow,
nor the fatherless, the stranger, nor the poor;
and let none of you imagine evil
against his brother in your heart.

— *Zechariah 7:9–10*

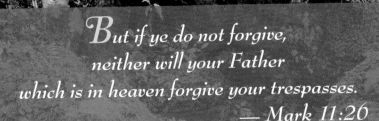

But if ye do not forgive,
neither will your Father
which is in heaven forgive your trespasses.
— Mark 11:26

Behold, I am the Lord, the God of all flesh:
is there any thing too hard for me?
— Jeremiah 32:27

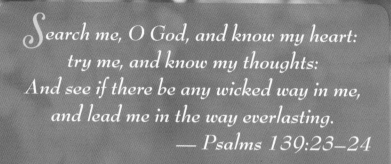

Search me, O God, and know my heart:
try me, and know my thoughts:
And see if there be any wicked way in me,
and lead me in the way everlasting.
— Psalms 139:23–24

What a rare combination: great advice that's
beautifully written. What does God find
when he searches you?

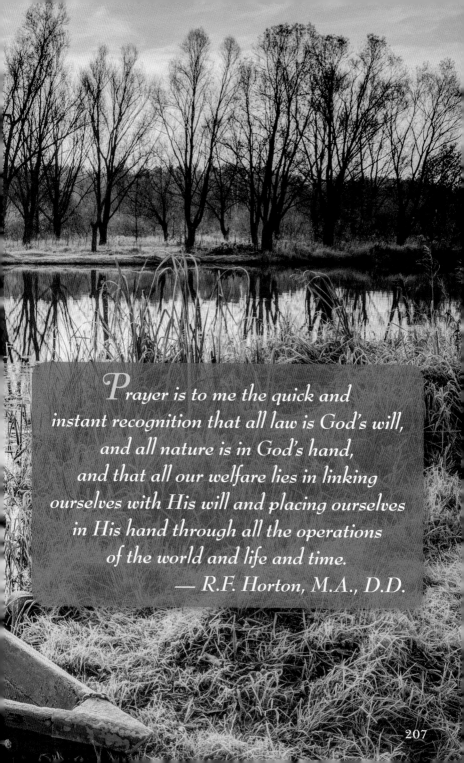

*Prayer is to me the quick and
instant recognition that all law is God's will,
and all nature is in God's hand,
and that all our welfare lies in linking
ourselves with His will and placing ourselves
in His hand through all the operations
of the world and life and time.*

— R.F. Horton, M.A., D.D.

*The bands that mothers and sisters
weave by prayer and precept
are the strongest in the world.*
                        — Mary Slessor

Then they cried unto the Lord
in their trouble, and he delivered them
out of their distresses.

— Psalms 107:6

$\mathcal{A}$s yet God suspends me between heaven
and earth, as a meteor; and I am not
in heaven because an earthly body clogs me,
and I am not in the earth
because a heavenly soul sustains me.
— John Donne

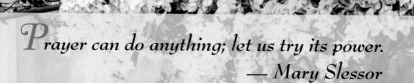

Prayer can do anything; let us try its power.
— Mary Slessor

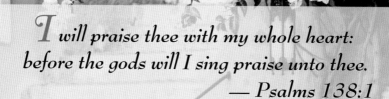

I will praise thee with my whole heart:
before the gods will I sing praise unto thee.
— Psalms 138:1

*But we are all as an unclean thing,
and all our righteousnesses are as filthy rags;
and we all do fade as a leaf;
and our iniquities, like the wind,
have taken us away.*

— Isaiah 64:6

To acknowledge humankind's nature as sinful beings, we must look frankly at ourselves; but we also have so much room to improve and strive and grow. A filthy rag is rinsed clean. A fallen leaf is replaced by a bright new bud. We walk against the wind until we reach home.

*In the day when I cried thou answeredst me,
and strengthenedst me
with strength in my soul.*

— Psalms 138:3

$\mathcal{N}$ow, indeed, if never before,
the heavens declared the glory of God.
It was to the full sky of the Bible, of Arabia,
of the prophets, and of the oldest poems.

— Walt Whitman

We are in face of a mystery.
A little humility and obedience
to revelation helps us out.
— W. Knox Little, M.A.

The prayerful soul must be sure that
"God is," and that he heeds the call
of his children.
— Russell H. Conwell

God is my Father, I am his child.
As truly as I delight to be sought for
by my child when he is cold or hungry,
ill, or in need of protection,
so is it with my Heavenly Father.
— Rosalind Goforth

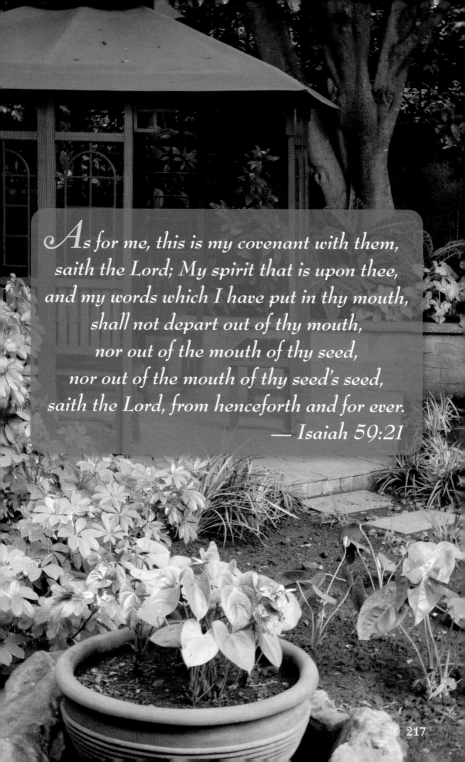

As for me, this is my covenant with them,
saith the Lord; My spirit that is upon thee,
and my words which I have put in thy mouth,
shall not depart out of thy mouth,
nor out of the mouth of thy seed,
nor out of the mouth of thy seed's seed,
saith the Lord, from henceforth and for ever.
— Isaiah 59:21

The moment I am assured that God hears me too, I feel drawn to pray and to persevere in prayer. I feel strong to claim and to take in faith the answer God gives.

— Rev. Andrew Murray

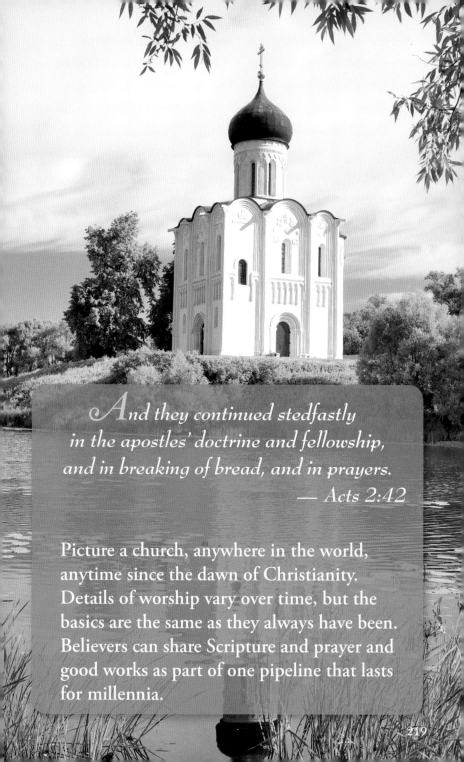

*A*nd they continued stedfastly
in the apostles' doctrine and fellowship,
and in breaking of bread, and in prayers.

— *Acts 2:42*

Picture a church, anywhere in the world,
anytime since the dawn of Christianity.
Details of worship vary over time, but the
basics are the same as they always have been.
Believers can share Scripture and prayer and
good works as part of one pipeline that lasts
for millennia.

Begin by setting apart some time every day,
say ten or fifteen minutes,
in which you say to God and to yourself,
that you come to Him now
as intercessor for others.
Let it be after your morning
or evening prayer, or any other time.
If you cannot secure the same time every day,
be not troubled.
Only see that you do your work.

— Rev. Andrew Murray

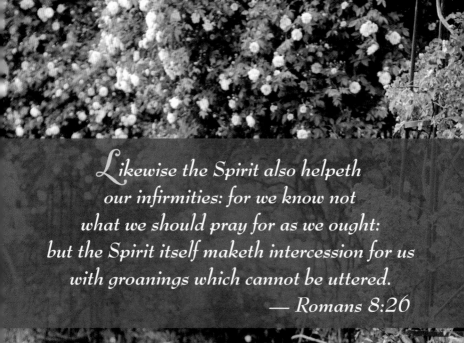

*Likewise the Spirit also helpeth
our infirmities: for we know not
what we should pray for as we ought:
but the Spirit itself maketh intercession for us
with groanings which cannot be uttered.*

— Romans 8:26

*And when they heard that, they lifted up
their voice to God with one accord,
and said, Lord, thou art God,
which hast made heaven, and earth,
and the sea, and all that in them is.*

— Acts 4:24

*O Lord, prepare the inhabitants
of the earth*

*To live in this world
and in the world to come.*
— *Nancy Luce*

*Hitherto have ye asked nothing
in my name: ask, and ye shall receive,
that your joy may be full.*
— John 16:24

Furthermore we have had fathers
of our flesh which corrected us,
and we gave them reverence:
shall we not much rather be in subjection
unto the Father of spirits, and live?
For they verily for a few days chastened us
after their own pleasure; but he for our profit,
that we might be partakers of his holiness.
— *Hebrews 12:9–10*

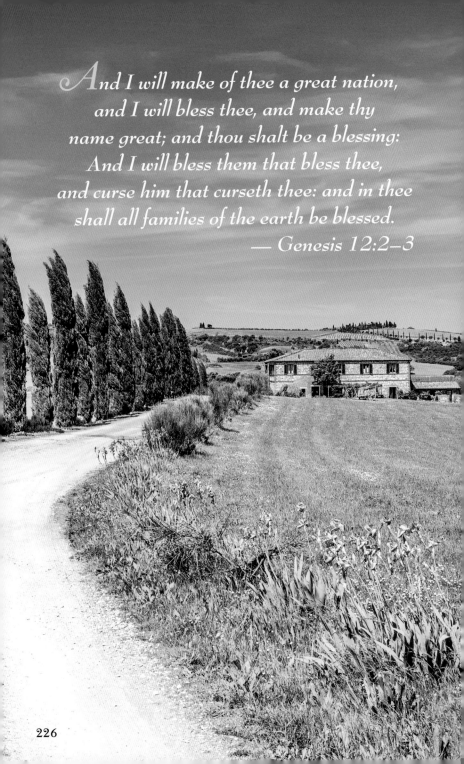

And I will make of thee a great nation,
and I will bless thee, and make thy
name great; and thou shalt be a blessing:
And I will bless them that bless thee,
and curse him that curseth thee: and in thee
shall all families of the earth be blessed.
— *Genesis 12:2–3*

Let, I pray thee,
thy merciful kindness be for my comfort,
according to thy word unto thy servant.
                          — Psalms 119:76

We live in God's world and were made in his image, which means we're surrounded by chances to use our own merciful kindness. Like a muscle, this quality thrives on heavy lifting.

*G*race be unto you, and peace,
from God our Father
and the Lord Jesus Christ.
We give thanks to God and
the Father of our Lord Jesus Christ,
praying always for you.
— *Colossians 1:2–3*

*And call upon me in the day of trouble:
I will deliver thee, and thou shalt glorify me.*
— *Psalms 50:15*

We think of God's mercy in a personal way
— that he is merciful to us flawed human
believers — but his mercy shines brightly
each time he asks his people to spread the
good word. With each new believer, God's
love multiplies.

What? know ye not that your body is the temple of the Holy Ghost which is in you, which ye have of God, and ye are not your own? For ye are bought with a price: therefore glorify God in your body, and in your spirit, which are God's.

— 1 Corinthians 6:19–20

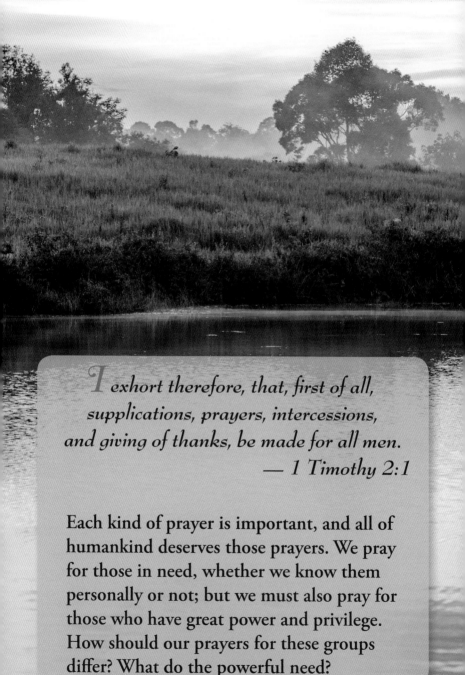

I exhort therefore, that, first of all, supplications, prayers, intercessions, and giving of thanks, be made for all men.
— *1 Timothy 2:1*

Each kind of prayer is important, and all of humankind deserves those prayers. We pray for those in need, whether we know them personally or not; but we must also pray for those who have great power and privilege. How should our prayers for these groups differ? What do the powerful need?

O Lord, open thou my lips;
and my mouth shall shew forth thy praise.
For thou desirest not sacrifice;
else would I give it:
thou delightest not in burnt offering.
The sacrifices of God are a broken spirit:
a broken and a contrite heart,
O God, thou wilt not despise.
— Psalms 51:15–17

*T*rue love must pray.
— Rev. Andrew Murray

*N*ow mine eyes shall be open,
and mine ears attent unto the prayer
that is made in this place.
— 2 Chronicles 7:15

233

But without faith it is impossible
to please him: for he that cometh to
God must believe that he is,
and that he is a rewarder of them
that diligently seek him.
— Hebrews 11:6

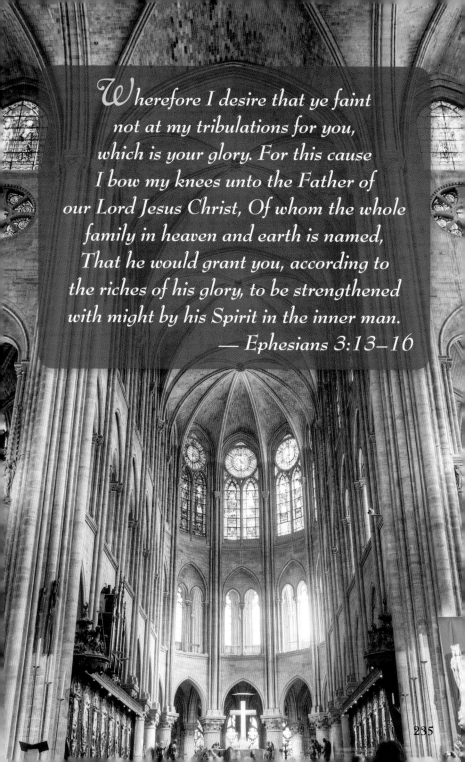

*Wherefore I desire that ye faint
not at my tribulations for you,
which is your glory. For this cause
I bow my knees unto the Father of
our Lord Jesus Christ, Of whom the whole
family in heaven and earth is named,
That he would grant you, according to
the riches of his glory, to be strengthened
with might by his Spirit in the inner man.
— Ephesians 3:13–16*

*G*od loves to give to them
who love to let Him have His way;
they find their happiness in the chime of
their own desires with the will of God.
— Theodore L. Cuyler, D.D.

*C*all unto me, and I will answer thee,
and show thee great and mighty things,
which thou knowest not.

— *Jeremiah 33:3*

*Let us yield ourselves to God to obey
His voice. Let no fear of past failure,
let no threatening array of temptations,
or duties, or excuses, keep us back.*
— Rev. Andrew Murray

Come, and let us return unto the Lord:
for he hath torn, and he will heal us;
he hath smitten, and he will bind us up.
— *Hosea 6:1*

God is the beginning and the end (Revelation 22:13), and throughout Scripture we see the ways in which he is the only action and reaction. Only God can tear us, and only God can heal us. When we feel torn, there's simply no other choice than to ask God for help.

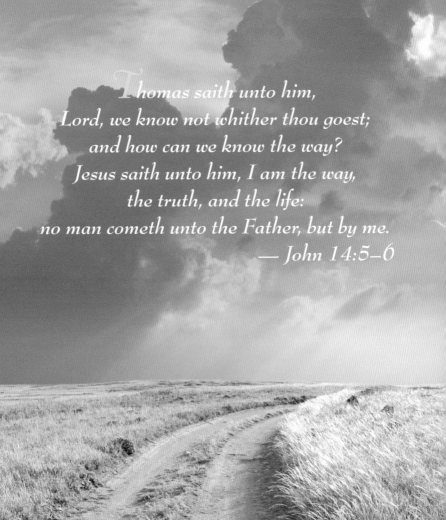

Thomas saith unto him,
Lord, we know not whither thou goest;
and how can we know the way?
Jesus saith unto him, I am the way,
the truth, and the life:
no man cometh unto the Father, but by me.
— *John 14:5–6*

Shall any teach God knowledge?
— *Job 21:22*

Then shall ye call upon me,
and ye shall go and pray unto me,
and I will hearken unto you.
— *Jeremiah 29:12*

How precious also are thy thoughts
unto me, O God! how great is
the sum of them! If I should count them,
they are more in number than the sand:
when I awake, I am still with thee.
— *Psalms 139:17–18*

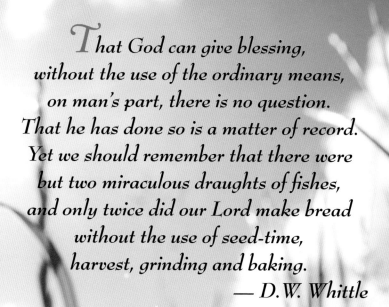

That God can give blessing,
without the use of the ordinary means,
on man's part, there is no question.
That he has done so is a matter of record.
Yet we should remember that there were
but two miraculous draughts of fishes,
and only twice did our Lord make bread
without the use of seed-time,
harvest, grinding and baking.

— D.W. Whittle

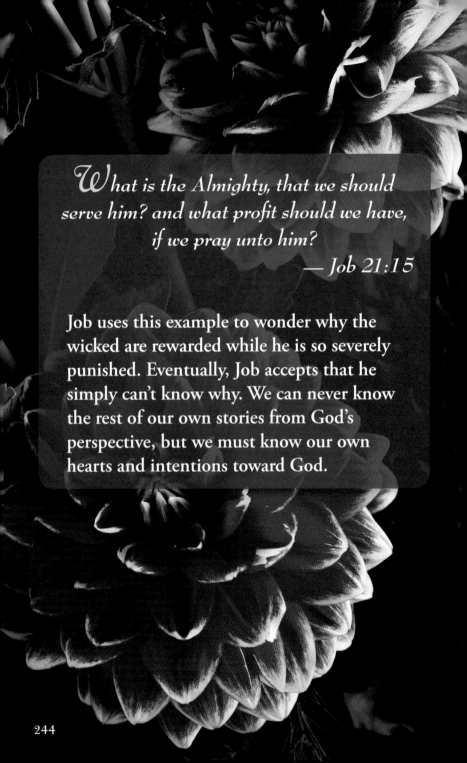

What is the Almighty, that we should serve him? and what profit should we have, if we pray unto him?

— Job 21:15

Job uses this example to wonder why the wicked are rewarded while he is so severely punished. Eventually, Job accepts that he simply can't know why. We can never know the rest of our own stories from God's perspective, but we must know our own hearts and intentions toward God.

*And when they had prayed,
the place was shaken
where they were assembled together;
and they were all filled with the Holy Ghost,
and they spake the word of
God with boldness.*

— *Acts 3:31*

O lord, thou hast searched me,
and known me.
— Psalms 139:1

Whoso stoppeth his ears at the cry
of the poor, he also shall cry himself,
but shall not be heard.
— Proverbs 21:13

If a son shall ask bread of any of you
that is a father, will he give him a stone?
or if he ask a fish, will he for a fish give him
a serpent? Or if he shall ask an egg,
will he offer him a scorpion?
If ye then, being evil, know how to give
good gifts unto your children:
how much more shall your heavenly Father
give the Holy Spirit to them that ask him?
— *Luke 11:11–13*

I give myself unto prayer.

— Psalms 109:4

T rust in him at all times;
ye people, pour out your heart before him:
God is a refuge for us.

— Psalms 62:8

*Looking back on the way by which
we have come, it seems to me now
that faith and work necessarily go together.
Earnest believing prayer is not less earnest
and believing because you use the means
God has put within your reach.
Your dependence upon God is just the same.*
— Leonard K. Shaw

When they therefore were come together, they asked of him, saying, Lord, wilt thou at this time restore again the kingdom to Israel? And he said unto them, It is not for you to know the times or the seasons, which the Father hath put in his own power. But ye shall receive power, after that the Holy Ghost is come upon you.

— Acts 1:6–8

Be assured that if you begin,
God will help you.
God cannot help you
unless you begin and keep on.
— Rev. Andrew Murray

251

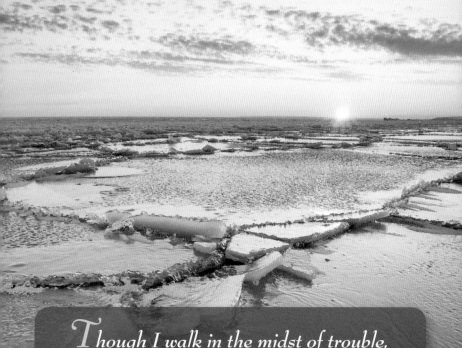

Though I walk in the midst of trouble,
thou wilt revive me:
thou shalt stretch forth thine hand
against the wrath of mine enemies,
and thy right hand shall save me.
— *Psalms 138:7*

This prophetic psalm reminds us that Jesus Christ is at the right hand of God, using our enemies as his footstool (Hebrews 10:13). The revival is literal, but it's also spiritual. Repeating the verse is invigorating and powerful.

*Confess your faults one to another,
and pray one for another,
that ye may be healed.
The effectual fervent prayer
of a righteous man availeth much.*

— James 5:16

Sharing builds bonds and reduces our emotional burdens. It shows our friends and loved ones how much we value them. Is there any kinder gesture than a prayer of compassion and understanding?

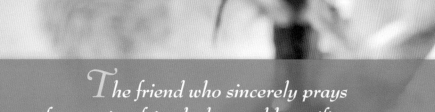

*The friend who sincerely prays
for you is a friend who would sacrifice most
for you in case of need.*
— *Russell H. Conwell*

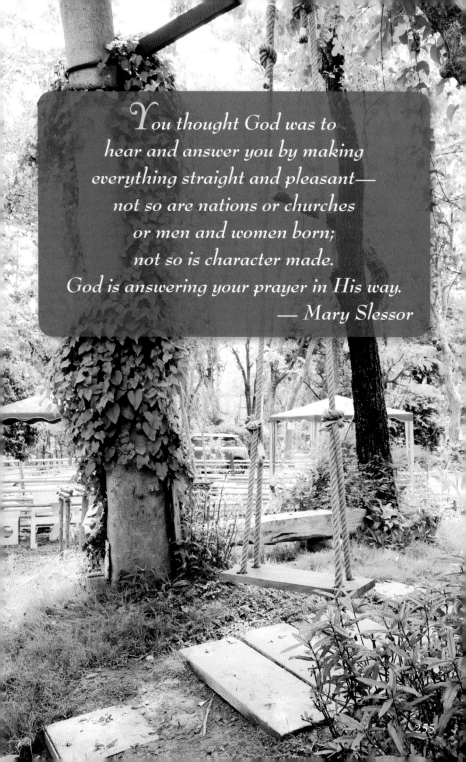

You thought God was to
hear and answer you by making
everything straight and pleasant—
not so are nations or churches
or men and women born;
not so is character made.
God is answering your prayer in His way.
— Mary Slessor

255

*And we have known and believed
the love that God hath to us.
God is love; and he that dwelleth in love
dwelleth in God, and God in him.
Herein is our love made perfect,
that we may have boldness in the day
of judgment: because as he is,
so are we in this world.*

— 1 John 4:16–17